West Africa

Word, Symbol, Song

West Africa

Word, Symbol, Song

edited by

Gus Casely-Hayford, Janet Topp Fargion and Marion Wallace

First published in 2015 by
The British Library
96 Euston Road
London NW1 2DB

On the occasion of the British Library exhibition
West Africa: Word, Symbol, Song
16 October 2015–16 February 2016

British Library Cataloguing-in-Publication Data
A catalogue record for this book is available from the British Library

ISBN 978 0 7123 0989 9

Designed by Andrew Shoolbred
Picture research by Sally Nicholls
Printed in Italy by Printer Trento

Picture acknowledgements

a = above, **b** = below, **l** = left, **r** = right

14 Courtesy of Daniela Moreau/Arcervio Africa-São Paulo, Brazil; **18** © Nyamoi Fall Taylor; **27** "Sunjata: Warrior King of Mali" written by Justine and Ron Fortes, illustrated by Sandy Carruthers. Copyright © 2008 by Lerner Publishing Group, Inc. Reprinted with permission of Graphic Universe, a division of Lerner Publishing Group, Inc. All rights reserved; **28** Courtesy of Daniela Moreau/Arcervio Africa-São Paulo, Brazil; **34, 35** © Alexandra Huddlestone; **42** Kwasi Ampene; **52** © Alexandra Huddlestone; **68** Basel Mission/Mission Holdings; **79** Courtesy Mr Rami El Nimer; **88** © LOOK der Bildagentur der Fotografen GmbH/Alamy; **90** © Amelia Ayagoge/Alamy; **91** © Eye Ubiquitous/Alamy; **93** Analog Africa; **94** Lucy Durán; **95l** Library of Congress, Prints and Photographs Division, Washington, D.C.; **95r** © Ulf Jägfors; **96** Dave Peabody/Redferns/Getty Images; **104** Library of Congress, Prints and Photographs Division, Washington, D.C.; **108** Courtesy of the Hunter Family; **118** © Ken Saro-Wiwa Foundation and Ken Saro-Wiwa Jnr.; **122** © Lynn Taylor; **137** Eliot Elisofon/The LIFE Picture Collection/Getty Images; **145** © Tristram Kenton; **150a** John Prieto/The Denver Post via Getty Images; **150b** Demotix.

Contents

Pius Adesanmi is a Professor of English and African Studies at Carleton University, Ottawa, Canada. His book, *You're Not a Country, Africa*, won the inaugural Penguin Prize for African Writing in the non-fiction category.

Karin Barber is Professor of African Cultural Anthropology at the University of Birmingham. Her research focuses on Yoruba oral literature, popular theatre and print culture in Nigeria. She has also done comparative work on popular culture and textual production across Africa. Her recent publications include *The Anthropology of Texts, Persons and Publics* (2007) and *Print Culture and the First Yoruba Novel* (2012).

Dr Gus Casely-Hayford is a cultural historian, curator and broad-caster with a particular interest in Africa. He was the instigator and director of 'Africa 05', a season of more than a thousand Africa-related events hosted by more than 150 organisations. He has written widely on African history, and his book *Lost Kingdoms of Africa* was supported by two series of BBC programmes. He is currently working towards an exhibition that will explore portraiture through the lens of slavery and its abolition for the National Portrait Gallery. He lectures widely, being a trustee at the National Portrait Gallery, a member of the African Studies Association of the UK board and on the Caine Prize Council; he is a research associate at the Centre for African Studies, SOAS.

Lucy Durán is Senior Lecturer in African Music at SOAS and writes extensively on West African music and culture. She has a long professional involvement with the music industry, as music producer, journalist and broadcaster, notably as presenter of BBC Radio 3's world music programme *World Routes*. Her *Growing into Music* project resulted in several films documenting musical progress of children in leading Mande *jeli* (griot) families. She is also project advisor to the Aga Khan Music Initiative for their work in Mali.

Stephanie Newell is Professor of English at Yale University. Her research focuses on African literature and media. Her books include *Ghanaian Popular Fiction* (2000), *Literary Culture in Colonial Ghana* (2002), *West African Literatures: Ways of Reading* (2006), *The Forger's Tale* (2006) and *The Power to Name* (2013).

Insa Nolte is Reader in African Culture at the University of Birmingham and Vice President of the African Studies Association of the UK (ASAUK). Her current research explores the importance of everyday encounters and interpersonal relationships for relations between Muslims, Christians and followers of indigenous traditions in Southwest Nigeria.

Janet Topp Fargion is Lead Curator, World and Traditional Music at the British Library and is a curator of the British Library exhibition 'West Africa: Word, Symbol, Song'. She has published extensively on ethnomusicology and archiving and is author of *Taarab Music in Zanzibar in the Twentieth Century: A Story of 'Old is Gold' and Flying Spirits* (2014).

Marion Wallace is Lead Curator, African Collections at the British Library and a curator of the British Library exhibition 'West Africa: Word, Symbol, Song'. Her books include *A History of Namibia* (2011) and (edited with Terry Barringer) *DisConnects? African Studies in the Digital Age* (2014).

Acknowledgements

The editors are very grateful to the many, many people who have collaborated in this project and have contributed their most generous advice, encouragement, help and support to this book and the British Library's West Africa exhibition. Thank you – we could not have done it without you.

Members of the exhibition's advisory panel, chaired by Gus Casely-Hayford, have given generously of their time and advice. The members are: Moradeyo Adewunmi (Yoruba Arts Trust); Margaret Busby; Lucy Durán (SOAS, University of London); Dele Meiji Fatunla (Royal African Society); Jacinth Martin (Croydon Supplementary Education Project); Stephanie Newell (Yale University); Will Rea (University of Leeds); Sheila Ruiz (Royal African Society); Ade Solanke (Spora Stories); Arthur Torrington (Equiano Society); and Tricia Wombell (Black Book News).

We would like to thank Arik Air for generously providing flights to enable us to support our exhibition public events programme.

The many other people and organisations who have advised and supported us include: African Heritage Ltd (Olu Femiola); Jahman Anikulapo; Sally-Ann Ashton; Bukky Owoseni Ajayi; Ellah Allfrey; Karin Barber; Paul Basu; Dmitry Bondarev; Etienne Bryan; Amber Jane Butchart; Brycchan Carey; Business Council for Africa (Jonathan Howard); Baroness Lynda Chalker; Nenna Chuku; Makeda Coaston; James Currey; Morgan Dalphinis; Marine Defosse; Louisa Uchum Egbunike; Niyi Epega; Akachi Ezeigbo; Richard Fardon; Ian Foster; Graham Furniss; Aurélien Gaborit; Kadija George; Wangui wa Goro; Toby Green; Asha Hai;

Rebecca Jones; Charlotte Joy; Seraphin Kamden; David Killingray; Saran Keita; Rosemarie Marke; Alice Mayers; Murray Last; Tom McCaskie; Sophie Mew; Paolo de Moraes Farias; Paul Naylor; Okey Ndibe; Nigerian Community Waltham Forest (Debo Adewunmi); Otobong Nkanga; Anya Oed; Organisation of Young Africans (Firinne Ni Chreachain); Insa Nolte; Tunji Offeyi; Patrice Etienne; J. D. Y. Peel; Platform UK (Jane Trowell); David Pratten; Colin Prescod; Ranka Primorac; James Procter; Friederike Lüpke; Marie Rodet; Benedetta Rossi; Amanda Sackur; Minna Salami; Lola Shoneyin; Chris Spring; Wole Soyinka; Ola Uduku; Silvana Unigwe; Amanda Villepastour; Robin Walker; Ruth Watson; Zoe Whitley; Trevor Wiggins; and David Zeityln.

The process of assembling loans and audio-visual and graphic material for the exhibition and the book was greatly assisted by the advice and practical support of numerous people and institutions, including: Obed Abbey-Mensah; Peter Adler; Kwasi Ampene; Karin Barber; British Museum (especially Julie Hudson and Fiona Savage); Margaret Busby; Duncan Clarke; Bernard Collet; Lucy Durán; Endangered Archives Programme and grant-holders; Paulo de Moraes Farias; Juno Fitzpatrick; Ed Fordham; Rob Francis; Gordon Frimpong; Gallery of African Art; Jill Godwin; John Godwin; Horniman Museum, London (especially Margaret Birley and Johanna Zetterstrom-Sharp); Alexandra Huddleston; Insa Nolte; John Picton; Daniel Pierre Jatta; Michael Katakis; Ben Mandelson; Mission 21 (Anke Schürer and Claudia Wirthlin); Ray Mahabir; Carol McLeod; Amir Mohtashemi; Daniela Moreau; Carole Myers; Obiageli Okigbo; Marcia Ostashewski; National Centre for Arts and Culture, The Gambia (Alieu Jawara); Mary Nooter-Roberts; Pearson (especially Lesley Wilson); Pitt Rivers Museum, University of Oxford (especially Jeremy Coote and Christopher Morton); Will Rea; Allen F. Roberts; Eli Rosenblum; Ken Saro-Wiwa; Rikki Stein; Nyamoi Fall Taylor; Lynn Thomas; Ola Uduku; and the University of Birmingham Library Special Collections (especially Sarah Kilroy).

The exhibition curators, Janet Topp Fargion and Marion Wallace, were enormously helped and supported in their visit to Nigeria in March 2014 by staff members at the following institutions and organisations: Ake Arts and Book Festival; British Council (Lagos and London); British Museum; Committee for Relevant Art; Centre for Black and African Arts and Culture; Ford Foundation; National Museum, Lagos; Nsibidi Institute; and University of Ibadan; and by the following individuals: Al-Haji Chief Olanrewaju Adepoju; Bibi Bakare; Chief Mrs Nike Davies-Okundaye; Stephanie Newell; Eunice Offeyi; and Prince Eji Oyewole.

Last but not least, we would like to thank the many members of staff at the British Library who have committed so much time, effort and goodwill to this project.

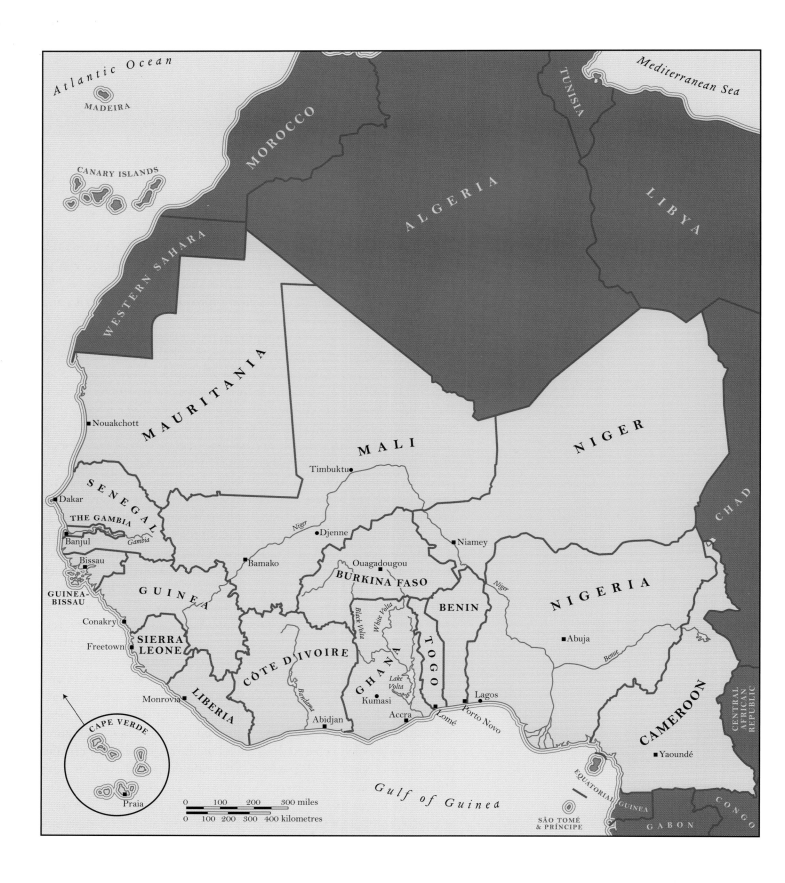

Atlantic Ocean

MADEIRA

CANARY ISLANDS

Mediterranean Sea

MOROCCO

TUNISIA

WESTERN SAHARA

ALGERIA

LIBYA

MAURITANIA

Nouakchott

MALI

NIGER

CHAD

Timbuktu

SENEGAL

Dakar

THE GAMBIA

Banjul

Gambia

Niger

Djenne

Niamey

Bissau

Bamako

Ouagadougou

NIGERIA

GUINEA-BISSAU

GUINEA

BURKINA FASO

Niger

Conakry

Black Volta

White Volta

BENIN

Abuja

SIERRA
LEONE

Freetown

CÔTE D'IVOIRE

GHANA

TOGO

Benue

Monrovia

LIBERIA

Bandama

Kumasi

Lake
Volta

Lagos

CAMEROON

CENTRAL AFRICAN REPUBLIC

CAPE VERDE

Abidjan

Accra

Lomé

Porto Novo

Yaoundé

Praia

0   100   200   300 miles

0 100 200 300 400 kilometres

Gulf of Guinea

SÃO TOMÉ
& PRÍNCIPE

EQUATORIAL GUINEA

GABON

CONGO

INTRODUCTION

GUS CASELY-HAYFORD
JANET TOPP FARGION
AND MARION WALLACE

This book accompanies a major exhibition on West Africa at the British Library, and brings together scholarship by a raft of experts in their fields to further interpret the exhibition themes. The exhibition was born out of an aspiration to celebrate the wealth and depth of West Africa's written heritage, and counter the idea that Africa is not, and was not, a literate continent. But, simultaneously, it also demonstrates the complexity, diversity, sophistication and flexibility of oral literature, sung and spoken – orature, as it is sometimes called – as a vessel for the creativity of African authors and musicians over past centuries and today. In addition, the exhibition shows the vast inventiveness of writers from West Africa as they turned to the medium of print, whether as creative, political or religious authors.

The exhibition and the book tell the story of West Africa in word, symbol and song. All these forms of creativity are well represented in the British Library's collections, which include manuscripts and maps, sound and video, and historical and contemporary publications from West Africa. In the exhibition and the present volume, these items are augmented by a wide variety of other objects – textiles, artefacts bearing symbols, masks, contemporary artworks – which contribute to the story of West African literature and orature from the distant past to the present day. We deal with history, literature, music and politics through five themes: precolonial Africa; religion; transatlantic connections; political, social and moral engagement; and contemporary creative literature.

Most would accept that the history of African literature and oral tradition is an area of intellectual achievement that has lain unacknowledged, and underappreciated, for too long; it has been unjustifiably overlooked and the accomplishments of its key figures have in large part been obscured by a long history of misunderstandings, misconceptions and prejudice. The West's long fascination with African cultures was so often a search for cultures that were like its own – since the classical era, European intellectuals have looked to Africa for buildings, material culture and intellectual achievements that were similar or comparable to the accomplishments of the cultures of

Map of West Africa, 2015.

These pottery inkpots, from different areas of West Africa, show the importance of writing and manuscript cultures to different ethnic groups. The top two pots feature penholders.

Top left:
Kano, Nigeria. Collected 1910–11.
Pitt Rivers Museum, University of Oxford.

Top right:
Niger. Collected 1922.
Pitt Rivers Museum, University of Oxford.

Bottom:
Northern Nigeria. Collected c. 1946.
Pitt Rivers Museum, University of Oxford.

Europe. They sought what Enlightenment thinkers, such as Immanuel Kant, later described as 'architectonic' bodies of knowledge, complex cultural superstructures with their own intellectual provenance. They looked for writing traditions like those that underpinned classical European cultures – and yet, as Kant and many other intellectuals of the Enlightenment claimed, they could not find them. The philosopher Georg Wilhelm Friedrich Hegel concluded that Africa 'as far as History goes back, has remained – for all purposes of connection with the rest of the World – shut up; it is the Gold-Land compressed within itself, – the land of childhood, which lying beyond the day of self-conscious history, is enveloped in the dark mantle of Night'.[1] Like many of his contemporaries, Hegel conjectured that as Europe emerged into light the African continent had been left locked in a culture-free state resembling Europe's dark and distant past.

And to some degree Euro-American cultures remain caught in the web of that Enlightenment-era misapprehension, a belief that Africa south of the Sahara had little of intrinsic cultural and intellectual merit and that it was a continent that somehow sat utterly isolated, beyond the reach of the European academy or the intellectual traditions of the eastern Mediterranean. It is a pervasive, enduring error to think that writing, that intellectual and philosophical traditions, were advances introduced by others to a seeming blank canvas, a precolonial continent devoid of formal history. This is a misconception that needs to be remedied. Africa was at no point shut up and isolated. Some of the great intellectual breakthroughs of the pre-Enlightenment age were made with contributions from African scholars, whose knowledge had been developed and nurtured in African centres of learning. These were intellectual traditions that Europeans sometimes found difficult to interface; this was an academy that was not always

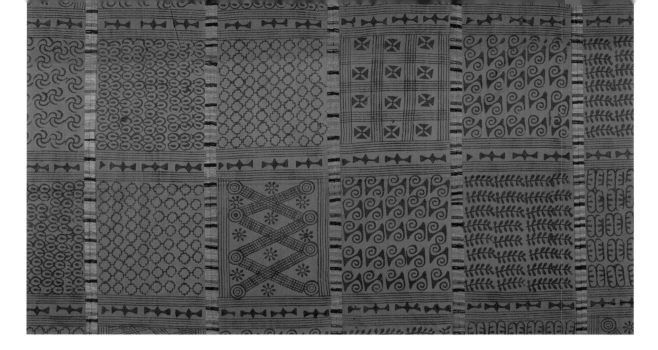

This is an example of *adinkra* cloth from Ghana, showing one of West Africa's many symbolic systems for encoding and communicating knowledge.

Ghana. ?1960s.

British Library.

This drum was bought from a Hausa trader near Ibadan in Nigeria in the 1950s. It is likely to be a kalangu used to 'speak' praises on special family and official occasions. The construction is almost identical to the more well-known Yoruba dùndún drum.

Horniman Museum.

physically located, or that could not consistently be identified by large bodies of written texts (as we shall see in Chapter 1). This was an intellectual culture that was in part located in the realm of music and popular stories, as well as in written scholarly culture. It was a set of conventions that had to operate in popular parlance, and when necessary they needed to yield substantive truths.

Writing came early to Africa. In West Africa, the Tifinagh script was in use among the Tuareg or Tamasheq, a Berber-speaking nomadic people living on the edges of the Sahara Desert, as long ago as a millennium and a half. With the arrival of Islam – first brought south across the Sahara in the 7th and 8th century – the Arabic language and script began to be adopted in West Africa, and scholarly cultures developed across the region in religion, theology and a multitude of other subjects including literature and law. The Arabic script was also widely used for the writing of West African languages such as Wolof and Hausa (a practice known as *ajami*).

West Africa is also rich in other means of encoding, preserving and communicating knowledge (or indeed rendering such knowledge the secret of a privileged few). Such methods include symbolic systems such as the beautiful *adinkra* and *nsibidi*; techniques of communicating messages in tonal languages through music – using drums, but also other instruments such as flutes and whistles; or the use of objects as mnemonics as in, for example, the àrokò system, in which a collection of shells and seed-pods could offer peace between kingdoms (as we shall see in Chapter 4). We cannot date these symbolic systems, but some of them may be very old; whatever their age, they, as well as the scholarship described above, are a testimony to the powers of inventiveness and creativity of African authors, musicians and makers over the centuries. And when European languages, the Roman script and

Collection Générale Fortier, Dakar

This picture of a *griot* (musician and storyteller) and his *kora* (calabash harp) was taken by Edmond Fortier, a photographer who spent nearly thirty years working in West Africa, mainly Senegal, in the early 20th century.

Private collection.

the printing press arrived on the coast of West Africa, it was African authors who took up these tools and used them in new, creative and challenging ways.

The coming of Christianity, as we shall see in Chapter 2, saw a large-scale effort to write African languages down in Roman script, and to codify and interpret them. Such an effort had to be large-scale because of the huge range of different languages in the region. West Africa today has more than a thousand languages, ranging from those like Bamanan, Hausa, Igbo, Pulaar, Wolof and Yoruba spoken by millions to those known only by a few thousand people. Human language in the region is very old: the Niger–Congo grouping, one of the major categories in West Africa, was in existence 15,000 years ago. Languages brought from outside also play a very significant role. Arabic, which arrived with Islam, has been spoken and written in West Africa for well over a millennium, and more recently the languages

This picture of Kofi Jatto performing phrases of text on Asante *atumpan* drums in Ghana in 1921 was taken by Robert Sutherland Rattray, an anthropologist and early adopter of the phonograph recorder.

Royal Anthropological Institute.

of colonialism, English, French and also Portuguese, have become very influential and are widely spoken and written; often, they are used for official and everyday communication in countries that have a wide variety of indigenous languages. Pidgin and Creole languages have also developed from contact between speakers of European and African languages, and are widely used.

If language itself goes back millennia in West Africa, then the oral literatures of the region are also of great antiquity. West African oral tradition is made up of a wide range of sophisticated forms that capture and document history, values and memory while also expressing creativity, invention and innovation, just as one would expect from any literary tradition. Proverbs, tales, epics and poetry are performed in a vast array of contexts and styles including storytelling, heightened speech (such as forms of praise poetry), drum and other instrument language (speech surrogacy) and song. Such oral litera-

Sorrow Tears and Blood
by Nigerian musician Fela
Anikulapo Kuti was originally
released in 1977 and comments
on the army raid on his home
on 18 February of that year. The
artwork is by Lemi Ghariokwu,
who designed covers for many of
Fela Kuti's records.
British Library 1LP0236386.

tures have always existed in West Africa and, despite changing times, continue into the 21st century through transmission from generation to generation as live performance – each new performance bringing to bear an artist's own creativity, world view, invention and adaptability. Mory Kanté's and Salif Keita's 1980s versions of the Malian Epic of Sunjata[2] are iconic renditions of this tale of the 13th-century foundation of the Mali empire, played with modern dance-band instrumentation, and exist alongside performances by today's griots (West African storytellers/praise singers/poets/musicians) on traditional instruments such as the *balafon* (xylophone) and *kora* (calabash harp).

In some ways it is the changing times that have assisted in keeping traditions alive. The invention of recording technology, and the employment of such early technology to document oral tradition, have enabled oral performance to be captured and disseminated, both within communities – through the ubiquitous 'market tapes'[3] of epics, stories and tales sold on cassettes and now on CD in market stalls throughout West Africa, which act as the oral tradition's equivalent of the book, bought, listened to and shared – and abroad, bringing knowledge, history and creativity to a global audience.

Throughout the 20th century, music and musicians have travelled abroad and returned to create wholly new musical styles that continue to act as part of West Africa's literatures, imparting commentary on social values and morals and acting as protest. They speak out in public about social and political conditions, from issues of women's rights, advocated by the likes of the Malian singer, Oumou Sangaré to the protest music of Fela Anikulapo Kuti, to socially motivated and educational rap music from Dakar – all drawing on proverbs, tales, epics and poetry, just as West African written literature does, in the popular domain.

This project could have taken the whole of Africa as its canvas. Magnificent examples of early scripts came from Egypt and Ethiopia; Arabic writing spread to many parts of the east as well as the west of the continent; 19th-century elites took up the printed word in the south; and oral literatures flourished everywhere. But these are large themes and spaces for a single project, and we believed the reader would be better served by a narrower – though still broad – focus on the history, literature, politics and music of a specific region. West Africa has great richness in all the fields discussed here, whether Arabic manuscripts, invented scripts, oral literatures or modern creative writing. It also has a particular connection with both old and new diasporic communities in the United Kingdom, the site of the exhibition, whether they have roots in the Caribbean and 'the black Atlantic', to use Paul Gilroy's famous phrase,[4] or in West Africa itself. The exhibition (as we shall see in Chapter 3) shows some of the routes by which people and expressive cultures reached Britain, the Caribbean and the Americas, and in some cases circled back again to Africa – and how individuals in this diaspora, as they did in Africa, turned literacy in English into rich means of self-expression.

We have taken here a broad definition of West Africa, stretching from Mauritania in the northwest to Cameroon in the southeast, and also including Benin, Burkina Faso, Cape Verde, Côte d'Ivoire, Guinea, Guinea-Bissau, The Gambia, Ghana, Liberia, Mali, Niger, Nigeria, Senegal, Sierra Leone and Togo. Of these countries, Nigeria today has by far the largest population – variously estimated at between 150 and 180 million – followed by Ghana, Cameroon and Côte d'Ivoire, with between 20 and 27 million each. The remaining countries, although some are very big in land area, have smaller – but rapidly growing – populations. We have not, of course, attempted to tell the story of all these countries in detail (and the reader should also keep in mind that the existence of most of them is a result of European division of African land in 1884–5, and in many cases bears little or no relation to the precolonial histories of the people of these territories). What we have sought to do is to tease out stories of people, of literatures, of cultures that illuminate both particular and general histories. And we have endeavoured to tell these stories using the British Library's collections, which are strongest for the former British colonies, partly because of the existence of colonial legal deposit, which meant that, during the colonial era, one copy of every item published in British

The Great Mosque at Djenné,
Mali, undergoing repair work.
Photographed by Nyamoi Fall
Taylor in June 2010.

colonies was to be donated to the Library of the British Museum.[5] Although often more honoured in the breach than the observance, this law nevertheless helped to lay a bedrock for the British Library's collections, which have also been augmented through donation and purchase. The British Library's holdings do, however, extend right across West Africa, and, wary of an anglophone viewpoint, we have calibrated our selections of objects to offer a broad and rich picture of the whole region.

This history of West Africa needs to be understood in relation to its ecology. The region consists of four broad climatic zones, running east–west. The northernmost is the Sahara Desert, which divides West from North Africa, but through which, along well-trodden desert routes, traders and travellers have circulated between the two regions for many centuries; the desert has been a significant means of, as well as a barrier to, communication. South of the Sahara is the Sahel, dry and in places semi-desert, in which the modern countries of Senegal, Mali, Mauritania and Niger are wholly or partly located. It was in the Sahel that West Africa's earliest known cities and empires emerged.

This illustration of a Songhai village appears in the work of Heinrich Barth, who travelled in West Africa in the mid-19th century. This picture post-dates the height of the Songhai empire's power, which declined after the Moroccan conquest in 1591.

British Library ORW.1986.a.786.

Djenné-jeno (old Djenné in modern Mali) was founded at least 2,500 years ago. The empire of ancient Ghana (from which the modern country of Ghana, though geographically distant, took its name) emerged at the latest in the 7th century. The Mali empire supplanted it in the 13th century, giving way in its turn to the Songhai empire, which, after a high point in the 15th–16th centuries, was displaced by Moroccan conquest and short-lived occupation. To the east and north, the Kanem-Borno empire endured from the 9th to the 19th century in parts of what is now Nigeria, Niger and Chad. From the 15th century, too, strong Hausa-speaking city-states emerged between the River Niger and Lake Chad; they were brought down by military campaigns that resulted in the foundation of the Islamic Sokoto Caliphate in 1804–08. The Caliphate expanded, comprising around thirty emirates at its height, and lasted for a century.

To the south of the Sahel lie the savannah and then the rainforest zones, and beyond them the Atlantic Ocean. Here the climate is much wetter and the land more fertile. Much of the history of these regions is that of the efforts of communities to carve a living out of the forest in one of the world's most difficult disease environments. Early states in these areas included Ife, a well-built city by at least the 14th century, and Benin, in existence from at least the 15th century (both were located in what is now Nigeria; the modern country of Benin is different from the old kingdom of that name).

Many West African states produced sculptures and other work of stunning artistry; those of Ife and Benin are among the best known. The time-depth of these empires, kingdoms and city-states helps to underline the antiquity of much written and oral literature in the region. When we look, for instance, at the great Epic of Sunjata (discussed in Chapter 1) the fact that this heritage extends back over many centuries becomes clear.

In contrast, European influence in West Africa is a relatively recent phenomenon. Europeans first appeared off the coast in the 15th century, but the transatlantic trade in enslaved people which they initiated and prosecuted did not reach substantial proportions for two centuries thereafter, peaking in the 18th century. Some of the implications of these events for those transported halfway across the world are considered in Chapter 3. For West Africa, the coastal trade had profound consequences, as the quest for people to enslave and export led to war and depredation far into the interior. It influenced the collapse of some states, including the Jolof and Oyo empires in modern Senegal and southwestern Nigeria respectively, as well as contributing to the rise of others including Dahomey (modern Benin) and Asante (modern Ghana).

Before the 19th century, European possessions in West Africa were largely confined to the coastal enclaves granted to them by local kings and emperors. As the slave trade was outlawed, beginning in the early part of that century, Europeans began to penetrate inland, developing what they called 'legitimate commerce' and increasingly coming into conflict with African states. By the end of the century the entire region – with the exception of Liberia, a colony founded as a refuge for emancipated African Americans, which had been granted independence from America in 1847 – had been carved up by the European powers. By the 1920s, after Germany had lost its colonies, the Portuguese had possession of Guinea-Bissau and Cape Verde; Britain was the colonial power for Nigeria, Ghana, Sierra Leone, The Gambia and a small part of what is now Cameroon; and the rest had fallen to France.

The difficulties faced by local populations under colonial rule have been widely documented. While colonial power took different guises and varied in its harshness – and it could be very harsh, resulting in large-scale massacres, conquests and exploitation – it was always an authoritarian, racially based form of rule and was widely, deeply and increasingly opposed. Nationalist movements developed in many colonies, particularly after the Second World War. The French policy of assimilation – which by the late colonial period had resulted in the election of some African deputies to the Assemblée nationale in Paris – ultimately failed, and Guinea achieved independence in 1958, followed by France's other West African colonies in 1960. British policies of indirect rule, most famously applied in Nigeria, were equally unsuccessful in the long run, and Ghana became independent in 1957, followed by the other British colonies in the region a few years later. Portugal did not relinquish its African possessions until it went through its own revolution in 1974; Guinea-Bissau and Cape Verde became independent shortly thereafter. Each of these independence struggles was first fought through words, many of West Africa's most active anti-colonial activists being its writers, lawyers, newspaper owners and the spokespeople of the traditional leadership. One of the effects of colonialism was to undermine many customary forms of governance and its orature, but also to enable the development of a rich body of reflective literature. And it remains possible to trace across generations the place of record in the fight for freedom.

Post-colonial rule in West Africa, in many cases, dashed early hopes of development and prosperity; many of the newly liberated countries went through periods of dictatorship and civil war, as well as bearing the brunt of neo-liberal financial policies imposed by international institutions during the 1980s. Today, West Africa is, on the whole, more stable and more democratic than in the past, although the narrative of 'Africa rising' has been partly undermined by new challenges from climate change, Islamist insurgency and, in 2013–15, the virulent outbreak of Ebola virus disease (which mainly afflicted Sierra Leone, Liberia and Guinea). But perhaps the bigger pervading narratives are of dynamism, of the lives of the vast majority having been affected by a deeper wave of economic growth, increasing cultural confidence and technological advances. This exhibition, and thus this book, is about the enduring expressive cultures of a vast, diverse, sophisticated and globally connected region of the world as they have tracked across periods of profound political and economic change. Throughout West African history, people's stories, and collective memories and narratives, have continued to emerge in writing, and as visual art and music – in word, symbol and song. New generations continue to find new ways of reinvesting in narrative, of using film and digital technologies to help reconsider traditional themes, and helping us reimagine the West African future.

Endnotes
1   Georg Wilhelm Friedrich Hegel, *The Philosophy of History* (New York: Dover, 1956), p. 91.
2   Published on side A and B, respectively, of Syllart Records SYL 8357 (1988).
3   Described by David Conrad in *Epic Ancestors of the Sunjata Era: Oral Tradition from the Maninka of Guinea* (Madison: African Studies Program, University of Wisconsin, 1999).
4   Paul Gilroy, *The Black Atlantic: Modernity and Double-Consciousness* (London: Verso, 1993).
5   This collection forms the core of the modern British Library.

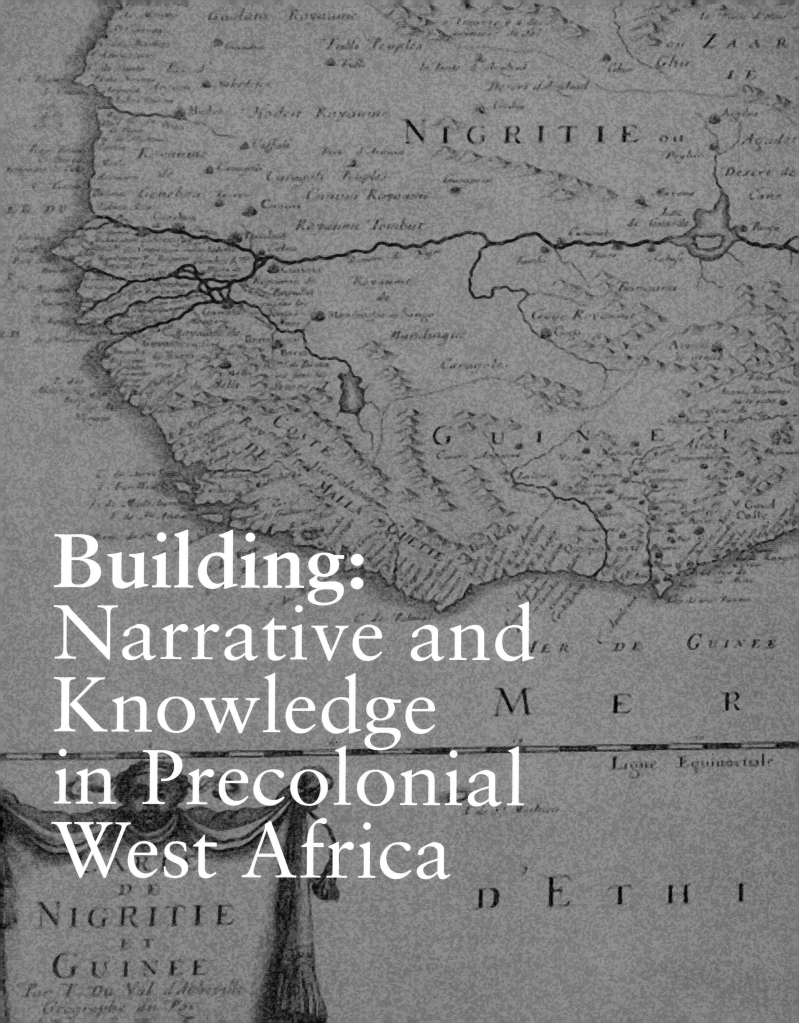

Building:
Narrative and
Knowledge
in Precolonial
West Africa

GUS CASELY-HAYFORD

When in the early 16th century the French writer François Rabelais wrote that 'you know well that Africa always brings something new'[1] he was alluding to a truly ancient European adage, a sentiment once used by thinkers such as Aristotle and Pliny, a belief that Africa was afflicted not just with a perversely overwhelming natural and cultural diversity, but also with a formidable and disturbing capacity for cultural invention. Even though the great medieval African centres of learning (like Ethiopia, Morocco and Mali) had over centuries had an impact upon culture across Europe and the Middle East, earning real respect for African innovation and thinking, many Europeans shared with Rabelais a feeling that Africa was fascinating, but somehow all too strange. Then with the Enlightenment came a profound hardening of that attitude towards Africa. For many European intellectuals, Africa, rather than being a curiosity, was something of a thorny problem. Although Africa lay in close proximity, it somehow seemed culturally distant and singularly challenging to interface. When they sought cultural exchange they found that the African academy was not always physically located, and could not always be identified by large bodies of written texts. In a period when taxonomies, hierarchies and bodies of writing became a European cultural obsession, as new categories were being force-fully developed to make sense of a rapidly changing world, it was easy to close the door on the African cultural conundrum, to system-atically disregard the continent's contribution to intellectual devel-opments and to place Africa at the bottom of the list of continents, beyond serious consideration.

Yet the dialectical conventions that underpinned Europe's Enlightenment – the positing of theses and counter-arguments, the synthesizing of multiple narratives, the value given to history, teaching and convention – were all also traditionally strong facets of West African cultures. But there was undoubtedly also a differ-ence: West African intellectual culture readily accepted that great ideas could also develop and reside beyond the formal academy within the wider cultural ambience, and be expressed through music, performance, storytelling or recitation. This was a system of learning that often distilled and diffused big ideas to make them engaging, elegant and accessible. It was a set of West African customs that were conceived to be effective in winning over hearts and minds in making an impression on the very young and the very influential alike, and yet when necessary were robust enough to support and yield substantive truths. Its elegant intellectual axioms could lie seemingly innocent and passive within the cultural ambience, flexible enough to adjust over time or within different contexts, yet always there when needed to support robust intellectual planks around which forceful identity politics could coalesce. Stories were the mechanisms through which many ideas found form, the mechanisms for preserving and promoting shared ideas and values: they could be beautifully robust anchors, or potentially caustic, divisive and incendiary. That web, the cultural fabric of words, created a somewhat ineffable, but formidable, intellectual infrastructure. Even today it remains possible to twitch what might seem an insignificant thread on the edge of the vast nexus of West African narrative activity and to see reverberations run broad and deep. Stories remain alive and contentious – seemingly humble narratives continue to be the focus around which many communities cohere, and through which they can be undermined – and the possibility that societies can through narrative be made or unmade remains vividly ever-present.

Shared Stories

It is quite understandable why, when Europeans such as Rabelais sought similarities with what they knew in Europe, they were frustrated by Africa. What they perceived as the African cultural void was in actuality a robust system driven by dynamic engagement, a system that could accommodate difference and even certain kinds of revolutionary act. According to Greek mythology, Prometheus stole fire from the gods. But Anansi the spider, the comic anti-hero of West African and Caribbean fable, was far, far more audacious: he sought from God the very fabric of conscious being, the element that would truly elevate him above other living things. This spider wanted the ingredient that was essential in binding peoples together and defining them, crucial to the building of states and the contesting of them: Anansi wanted *The Story*.

Anansi knew stories could be important; he understood that shared stories are critical to functioning societies. Yes, fire was fundamental, but when we gathered around hearths it was so often stories that drew us there, and it was more often than not shared narrative that held us there. Stories helped us galvanise, evangelise and in some circumstances ostracise; they marked victor from vanquished, and were the foundation upon which humble families and great states were built. Stories were not just the intellectual confectionery of childhood, but the integral fabric of law, science and art. When paired with real power, stories were the bedrock of social order, the underpinning of a nation's identity.

Over the second half of 2012 dozens of Mali's most ancient monuments were deliberately damaged or destroyed. In a campaign of systematic vandalism, Ansar Dine, an Al Qaeda-affiliated militia, pushed further and further south from their Saharan strongholds into regions of deep historical importance, destroying tombs, damaging buildings and burning manuscripts. They eventually converged on Timbuktu. What happened next was more than vandalism or even an extreme form of iconoclasm: it was an attempt to deconstruct national identity by destroying Mali's totemic anchors of shared heritage.

At the time of the invasion Ansar Dine were a ragtag coalition of disaffected young men, aggrieved Tuareg rebels and religious militants armed with third-hand weapons liberated from the rapidly disintegrating Libya; yet despite varied causes and diverse backgrounds they were ardently united by Islam, and a potent understanding of what narrative could mean to people. They understood that stories could be vital building blocks of successful societies. As Anansi sought to leverage power through shared stories, Ansar Dine strove to challenge the status quo by destroying the most prestigious symbols of the broadly accepted narrative. Both relied upon revolutionary acts, the wresting of power from the accepted authorities, the challenging of established norms and an attempt to control the accepted story. Ansar Dine could look back across history at a number of potent precedents. In the face of seemingly unavoidable defeat, their audacious hope was that in cutting the knot that held the national narrative together, that nationhood would simply unravel. They hoped to strike at Mali's emotional and cultural heart, destroying Timbuktu's libraries, forbidding music, damaging the material culture and defacing the architecture; that is, to obliterate the physical embodiments of the nation's story in the hope that the old country would spiritually lose the will to be. In many ways it was not a naive ambition – stories are almost uniquely important for the people of this region. And the city that they were sacking was, and remains, the unquestioned fount of one of West Africa's most enduring chronicles.

In the first half of the 13th century the Mali empire was wrested from the shifting trade routes and societal chaos that were the fading embers of the once great Ghana empire. For almost a thousand years the Ghana empire had ruled over a vast region of what is today southeast Mauritania and western Mali. The demise of the Ghana empire presented an opportunity to found a new kind of state, led by a truly exceptional leader. Its founder, Sunjata Keita, was a formidable military strategist and visionary who, like so many great West African leaders that followed him, understood the importance of fashioning and securing his story. He wanted to be remembered as the man who consolidated the southern states of the once mighty Ghana empire into a coherent and ambitious new kingdom. And he would build upon those cultural and trading foundations created by the Ghana empire a deeply confident state that would dominate the region until the Songhai people conquered Djenné and Timbuktu to establish their own empire in the western Sahel over the course of the 15th century.

Sunjata had watched the last of the Ghana empire unravel, destabilised by the rise of Islam, compromised by the changing geography of trade and a contagion of internal disputes, and he must have long ruminated upon the fact that maintaining a state would be quite a different challenge from forging one. Perhaps he observed the potency of narrative within the increasingly popular Islam, had seen its ability to hold disparate peoples together, and he must have known from his upbringing how powerful and enduring West African oral tradition could be. Maybe he concluded that to make his citizens

The Epic of Sunjata has been told in many different ways. Ron and Justine Fontes transformed the tale into a modern graphic novel, *Sunjata: Warrior King of Mali*, published in 2011, which dramatically illustrates key episodes in the story.

British Library YK.2012.a.15026.

feel a sense of belonging and nationhood, they would have to share a story. We are forced to conjecture about the motives for the creation of the epic, but what we know is that Sunjata inspired one of the most beautiful West African tales ever crafted, an epic oral poem that would spread, and then sustain his magical status long after his death, and even after his empire had waned. The Epic of Sunjata is a story of the fearless forging of order from ambient chaos. Like Anansi and so many other central characters of West African stories, its protagonist and key focus is in many ways an unlikely, and initially unlucky, hero who overcomes a range of challenges to eventually prevail. At its heart lies the deep-rooted regional hankering for strong leadership and secure states, but also for the possibility of change.

Sunjata was the firstborn, disabled son of Sogolon, a magical hunchback princess, and King Maghan Konate, a dashing figure. From his birth Sunjata inspired prophesies that he would be the man who would one day unite the twelve kingdoms of Mali into a single unassailable entity. The people of the young, unstable, burgeoning Mali had seen the old Ghana empire implode, and they longed for a strong unifier. In Sunjata they hoped that they had found their king. But, as might be expected in a West African epic, fate was to play its hand. On the death of his father, the young Prince Sunjata did not ascend the throne. Usurped and pushed into exile by his younger brother and a rival queen, Sunjata was forced to watch from afar as his father's kingdom unravelled and neighbouring states became increasingly emboldened. Eventually, after a period of reflection in the wilderness, Sunjata could take it no longer. In fulfilment of the prophesies Sunjata reclaimed his rightful position, rebuilt his court, overcame Mali's adversaries and built an unrivalled empire that stretched across the savannah from the sea to the Sahara.[2]

Over years of retelling and centuries of reshaping, the Epic of Sunjata became an institution, recited often with musical accompaniment; its various oral versions evolved into potent mechanisms for reaffirming or challenging the importance of the Sunjata Keita dynasty and the Mali kingdom he founded. Part fable, part historical narrative, it was an odyssey that formed an anchor for the people of the growing state. It offered mythic scale and metaphysical nuance, and conveyed how the critical passages of their history were touched by destiny, and how its central anchoring figure was guided by something magical, perhaps divine.

And alongside Sunjata, a key figure in all the versions of the epic was the storyteller, the griot.[3] For societies in which stories were a vital cultural adhesive, the griots were enormously important. They helped build a particular tradition of histories underpinned with strong moral lessons. They could be entertaining, charming but also deadly serious; they were the custodians of the accepted narrative and keepers of the aristocratic genealogies and occasionally of uncomfort-

An Edmond Fortier postcard showing a griot, *c.* 1910.

Private collection.

JELLEMAN OF SOOLIMANA. JELLEMAN OF KOORANKO.

This is among the earliest published drawings of West African musicians and storytellers. It appears in Alexander Gordon Laing's account of his travels in an area that includes present-day Sierra Leone. Laing was also the first European to reach Timbuktu (in 1826), but died on his way back.

British Library G.2972.

able communal truths. Griots were aides and confidants of the royal court who somehow sat outside societal norms, able to comment on and analyse events with an irreverent wit and incisive accuracy. Their power was not just in the words, nor in the music that accompanied them, but as with Anansi, their knowledge and skill had also conferred a kind of magical status upon them. And the finest griots revelled in that difference, happy to reveal their disdain for everyday humdrum humanity and its frustrating inability to learn from history. Even today, they remain special figures, able to appear as characters in the very stories that they relate, to be part of the narrative while simultaneously constructing and delivering it, transcending the gap between past and present. The griots were special, and they knew it. They were not alone, however. State storytellers evolved within communities in similar but slightly varied form across much of West Africa. They were fundamental in helping to inculcate the idea of stories as the key cultural building blocks of thriving societies. From coastal Ghana, where they were called Okyaime ('he who makes it good for me'), to Northern Benin, where the oral narrators were Gesere, to Cameroon, where they took the name Gawlo, dozens of variants of official storytellers found critical roles in emerging societies. They were each custodians of their particular regional myths of origin, often stories of inspirational warrior kings who struggled against odds, like Sunjata, to fulfil their destiny of founding a kingdom. The saga of the powerful West African warrior-hero Ozidi became memorialised as songs, as stories, in performance, through material culture. It became a story that was owned by everyone, that could be remade to offer new relevance for new generations, that could migrate with peoples as West Africa's fluid demography shifted and changed over centuries. As these fledgling communities each grappled with their environmental and political challenges, they each in their own way recognised the importance of a founding narrative and the critical place that record would play in their futures.

The Epic of Sunjata, like other founding narratives, was successful not just because it was affecting and beautiful; it had a practical application of giving a root to a young, fragile community. In making sense of the founding of the Mali kingdom, it also became critical to maintaining it. Such stories created a foundation upon which law, tradition and chronology could be grafted. But these narratives also offered something else: while the epic was no doubt based on real events, it became through the retelling something other than just history. It was a cultural rallying point, a poetic parable around and through which people of the growing kingdom could identify. And over centuries it took on the mantle of an oral manuscript, ever fading, forever reconsidered and reconstructed, the ghostlike form of its earlier selves always somehow present; and the rhythms of the accompanying music burrow deep into the societal psyche to become an aural analogue for their kingdom's continuity. Even today these stories remain special.

Words Preserved in Text

Over the century that followed the development of the Epic, rather than fading from memory, the story of Sunjata became ever more embedded in hearts and minds. Each successive emperor – consolidating the regional dominance of the Mali empire, many moving and rebuilding the capital, most extending Mali's trading reach and

This image of Mansa (King) Musa, the Mali emperor (ruled 1307–?1332) comes from a Catalan atlas created in 1375, indicating that his fame had reached Europe.

Bibliothèque nationale de France.

broadening commercial relationships – added layer upon layer of narrative upon that founding mythology of Sunjata. Then in the early 14th century Mansa Musa, the tenth monarch, ascended the throne, heralding something utterly new, a period when Mali became unquestionably the most powerful kingdom in West Africa, and the nature of the state relationship to its narrative shifted once more.

Ibn Khaldun, the Arab Muslim historian, described something of this moment in his travel writings. One of a generation of Muslim intellectuals who first captured and translated the words of griots into written form, Ibn Khaldun fashioned an Arabic chronology of the many emperors who had sat on the throne of the Keita dynasty. As part of the generation who first transcribed Mali's oral history, he contributed to a moment when the state's relationship to history changed fundamentally. Ibn Khaldun witnessed the court of Mansa Musa, a perfect alignment of innovations in technologies, administration and diplomatic strategy and an exceptional head of state who understood the implications of what those advances could mean. Mansa Musa realised that written texts offered a chance to fix and further control narrative, and could be important mechanisms to challenge, perhaps defy, the characteristic fragility of oral histories. These were innovations in historical enquiry that would offer a longevity, perhaps even permanence, to the state narrative, countering the inherent ineffability and fluidity of oral histories, and giving the state history some of the same intellectual substructure as the scientific disciplines. It must have felt revolutionary to all who witnessed it. For the first time history was no longer ephemeral, poetic, intellectual gossamer; it had taken on a new kind of rigour. It was in many ways similar to Anansi's aspiration of corralling and containing all knowledge, and setting that learning to work towards particular ends. Mansa Musa would build one of the world's great libraries – and craft the intellectual substructure of an African Enlightenment.

And that written history has left us with a vivid picture of Mansa Musa, considered by many to have been the richest man in the medieval world, and perhaps the richest who has ever lived. Famed for his vast gold reserves and for sending envoys to the courts of Europe and the Middle East, he commanded a vast empire. He wanted to be seen as more than a playboy king, he sought more than the power and money that he had in abundance: he wanted wisdom and to be remembered as wise.

Perhaps the most vivid manifestation of that success is that today, we have all heard of Timbuktu. To many in the West an impossibly distant, romantic notion of a place, it is a city that is in actuality every bit as special as its magical reputation. A World Heritage Site, known as the 'City of 333 Saints', Timbuktu is the home of sixteen shrines of Sufis or Islamic saints and a place that like so many in West Africa was built upon stories. At its heart is not a palace, or a

This is a very early engraving of Timbuktu, published in 1830 by René Caillié, who in 1828 became the first European to reach the city and return alive.

British Library 10095.i.3.

fortified parliament, but a mosque, an ancient madrasa and one of the world's great libraries: buildings that make up the academic centre of Timbuktu. Originally constructed in or around 1327 out of earth and straw, underpinned by wood supports and limestone reinforcements, these structures hold one of the world's great libraries, and form an almost unique body of interpretations of Islamic texts.

Even though Timbuktu was the capital of the Mali empire, one of the richest trading empires Africa has ever produced, people were attracted to the city not just to trade, but because by the early 14th century it had forged itself into a world centre of learning. The magnificent adobe city on the edge of the Sahara had crafted itself into the centre of a very particular kind of education, focused on and driven by Islam. At its peak in the 16th century this institution was as influential and as innovative as any educational establishment in Europe, attracting 25,000 students in a city of only 100,000 residents. As much as this institution's reputation was based on its dazzling scholars, it also became famous for being a repository of books and manuscripts – thousands of texts, lovingly researched, written, copied, bound and preserved.

Africa boasts a number of magnificent ancient libraries that have offered the intellectual underpinning to some of its greatest empires and most forward-thinking leaders. And when set side by side with the magnificent Egyptian archives, the Ethiopian Berber Libraries or the document repositories of Mauritania or Hausaland, Timbuktu justifies a place among the very finest bodies of written historical material produced by intellectuals from across West Africa and the wider Islamic scholarly world. It is a vast and varied collection of more than 700,000 African documents, ranging from scholarly works to short letters, which have been preserved mostly within private libraries.

Before the 2012 invasion there were twenty-four private libraries in the city that held the bulk of the city's repository of manuscripts; some documents may date back to the period of the city's foundation in the 14th century. It is a collection that gives a unique window onto the scholastic development of this region. These were intellectually expansive and ambitious peoples who voraciously and liberally collected new and innovative thinking on a wide diversity of subjects, from algebra to cooking, from philosophical and theological tracts to essays and charts on the movements of the stars. This body of knowledge was used as the basis of law, of precedent for nuancing social and religious mores, and for making and sustaining intercontinental and international trading relations.

The library's threatened destruction in 2012 remains shocking. While the Malian army was not able to defend Timbuktu from the forces of Ansar Dine, their citizens made spirited attempts to protect their history, even at the risk of their own safety. Over weeks, archivists and their supporters evacuated manuscripts in cars, carts and canoes. They worked with taxi and bus drivers, hiding sheaves of materials among the baggage of the fleeing peoples. As one archivist said, 'little by little' significant sections of the great archives of Timbuktu were moved to safety. Some who could not make it south resorted to the truly ancient tradition, when under threat, of burying their precious collections in the desert. These were spontaneous and practical solutions that vividly demonstrated quite how important this body of material remains to the ordinary people of Mali.

In 1324 Mansa Musa went on a pilgrimage to Mecca. He was an emperor who travelled without compromise, making the journey accompanied by scribes and intellectuals, thousands of enslaved people and soldiers, wives and officials. It was recorded that among his retinue were 100 camels, each of which carried 100 pounds (more than 45 kilograms) of gold. And when his caravan stopped, it was as though a town had settled itself on the trade route, a town that would construct a fully functioning mosque each Friday of its journey. Mansa Musa performed so many acts of charity as his great caravan progressed across North Africa that as the great Berber chronicler,

The photographs above and opposite were taken by Alexandra Huddleston in 2007 in Timbuktu, Mali, where an ancient manuscript culture has survived into the present, despite past and recent conflicts in the area.

British Library Photo 1294 (7).

Imam Mahmoud Baba Hassèye with one of the manuscripts in his collection. Members of his family have been scholars and imams for generations.

British Library Photo 1294 (11).

Ibn Battuta, wrote, he 'flooded Cairo with his kindness', spending so much in the markets of North Africa and the Middle East that it affected the gold market well into the following century. And on his return, after indulging himself and his retinue of scholars at the great intellectual centres of North Africa and the Middle East, Mansa Musa memorialised his journey to Mecca by building an exemplary mosque, a library and a centre of learning in Timbuktu, the new heart of his empire. In many ways it set a new level of ambition for a centre of scholarship, and with its wealthy patron it could not only attract the most dazzling international scholars and thinking, but also develop an indigenous generation of intellectual talent that rivalled anything then known. It was as influential as the great European centres of learning developing in Salamanca, Oxford or Cambridge, and boasted its own great scholars, such as Ahmad Baba al Massufi.

Timbuktu's wealth and power initially grew because the city was the key hub on the most lucrative trans-Saharan trade routes. Berber merchants carried salt, textiles and new precious goods, along with learning, down into West Africa from across the desert. Where the cross-desert trade routes ended, a symmetrical nexus of trade routes followed the southward sweep of the River Niger carrying trade and ideas down deep into West Africa, and of course carried the new thinking back. During the reign of Mansa Musa the city grew to become a hub for ideas, looking beyond North Africa, southward at the trade and intellectual traditions of West, Central and Eastern Africa. Thus the growing Islamic intellectual traditions of Timbuktu not only sat on older West African tradition, but were also informed by new customs of Africa south of the Sahara. One of the city's greatest legacies is to quietly offer us an insight into that porosity of thinking: how African intellectuals from this region were part of the great medieval transcontinental academic debates and breakthroughs. Ideas initiated in the great centres of learning and mosques of Europe or the Middle East could find their own place in this city on the edge of the desert.

What Mansa Musa created became an exemplar for many other West African cultures. The fame of his wealth and the reputation of his library spread far and wide. It may have been his story that inspired the Christian fascination with the African Magus. This figure began to appear in medieval European painting in this period as a gold-bearing, learned African who journeyed from the south, carrying not just precious gifts but great wisdom. It is important to remember that in many ways Mansa Musa was not an anomaly. Although his love of written record and book learning was innovative for a head of state, his fascination with state narrative was not. He had formulated a different kind of West African monarchy, outward-thinking and in control of its written legacy, but it was based upon that ancestral imperative to control the communal narrative. But in using written texts alongside the oral testimonies of the griots, in giving the written record a formal status, or even precedence, he had conceived a template for new cultures developing along the gold traderoutes that cut down across West Africa.

The Early Impact of Europeans

The search for gold drove pioneering entrepreneurs further and further into the inhospitable forested regions to build new communities. Competing for resources and access to trade opportunities, these fledgling polities often fell victim to a fragile and highly fluid politics in which alliances were constantly being fostered and undermined. But where once this forested region was on the fringe of the

Map of West Africa, 1653. This map illustrates European knowledge of West Africa in the seventeenth century, and is not geographically accurate, since European activities were largely limited to the coast. It is particularly interesting for its representation of many African states, shown by castle-like symbols. The kingdom of Mali ('Royaume de Melli') appears many miles west of its actual heartland.

British Library Maps K.Top.117.86.

Saharan trade routes, the arrival of Europeans on the West African coast, and the development of a network of fortified coastal ports in the 16th century, transformed the status of these forest communities. Trade across West Africa opened up, with the establishment of new long-distance trade routes dissecting multiple regions, connecting states of varying scales from small and decentralised settlements of the forests to extensive, well-established empires of what are today Ghana, Nigeria and Cameroon. As trade routes began to link the gold-rich areas with the wealthy Hausa city-states, mobility of goods and people became possible in a way that was previously unimaginable. The centre of mercantile geography was aggressively pulled southward away from the Malian Sahel and the Niger Bend into densely vegetated and gold-rich regions. No longer at the end of trade routes, these communities relished the strategic benefits their place as middlemen brought to their control of the gold mines. Over the next three centuries this trade would transform the region and enable the

growth of a number of successful states, each brokering their own trading relationships with Europeans.

From the 17th century, European travellers, as hungry as their African peers, began to encroach on the inland trade, building new trading relationships to exploit what seemed a land of endless resource. To aid their compatriots and sponsors they heavily invested in charting the region, making surveys, and drawing and writing descriptions of what they saw. They painted pictures of a fluid and changing political landscape as a nexus of new communities emerged, and older cultures succumbed to the rapidly changing political geography and accepted the ascendance of a new order. Among those Young Turks were the Asante, who like the early Mali emperors seemed to relish establishing a new culture among the still-smouldering embers of a once-dominant rival. And by the turn of the 18th century, the Asante had turned a fragile foothold in the forests (of what is today Ghana's central region) into complete regional dominance.

'Adoom Street', as illustrated in Thomas Edward Bowdich, *The Mission from Cape Coast Castle to Ashantee*, 1819.

British Library G.7211.

If oral histories are to be believed the Asante state was born almost purely out of the force of will of its founding figures. Its first ruler, Osei Tutu, and his intellectual and spiritual guide, Okomfo Anokye, must have looked back across history for inspiration to the great medieval states such as Mali, but they also borrowed from their immediate neighbours as they forged their new kingdom.[4] They adopted and fostered goldsmithing traditions that were popular across the region and made them state trades. Goldwork took its place alongside cloth-printing and weaving traditions, and drum- and stool-making practices, that were given a special status. The Asante did not just exploit these trade skills for financial gain, or aesthetic benefit; they sought to invest and imbue these crafts with deep narrative resonance, nurturing within and through these artefacts a cultural reservoir of histories to underpin their new nation. They were determined to tie people with irresistible force to their new state, to pull their citizens deep into its story through symbols and traditions of the Asante royal court and their newly established shared myths of origin. And they sought out the most dazzling things to represent this sense of place and a connection to history.

Perhaps the most potent material symbol of the drive to connect people with the story of the state was the institution and promotion of family and state stools. Stools, like the great thrones of European monarchs, represented the authority of the monarchy and its continuity. For a people who sought rootedness, the Asante adoption of the stool was a perfect symbol of physical and emotional fixedness. The Asante royal family chose a stool of gold as the primary state symbol, and wove a story of how it descended from the skies to settle on Okomfo Anokye's lap. The golden stool was seen as too sacred ever

This black-and-white engraving, from a publication by Thomas Edward Bowdich, illustrates items of Asante culture with important symbolic associations. A sample of *adinkra* cloth is shown in the top right-hand corner, a stool in the bottom right and a sandal at bottom left.

British Library 800.k.3.

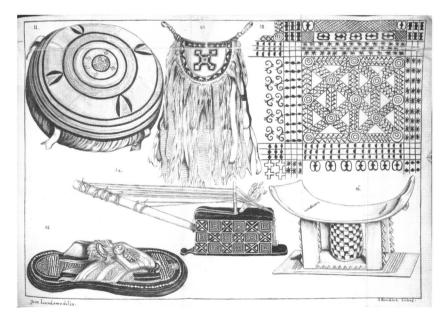

These are gold-weights, made of brass and used for weighing gold. These tiny sculptures are charged with symbolic meaning. The Sankofa bird indicates, among other things, the importance of history, and the golden stool is a symbol of kingship.

Ghana. 18th–20th century.

British Museum.

to be sat upon; it symbolised the initial blessing that underpinned the founding of the Asante kingdom. Very quickly, within and even beyond Asante territory, the symbol of the carved stool became seen as synonymous with history, with authority and genealogical connection. The stool took on a special, perhaps even supernatural, aura. This tradition inspired a very particular relationship to materials, and an understanding that narrative and a sense of temporal continuity could be wrapped into special objects. The golden stool and indeed a number of loved and venerated family stools became, over generations of possession, further altered, charged by that dynastic history.

The Asante understood, like their beloved Anansi, that history, that stories have an inherent power that can be harnessed and used. They even instituted a symbol, the Sankofa, a bird with its head turned backward, stretching to capture something out of reach. It represented their inherent cultural respect for the pursuit of history and state narrative, but was also an acknowledgement of the idea of historical enquiry being an active conscious thing that must be concertedly done by those in authority. That Asante reification of history was publicly satisfied and symbolised in a number of ways. Sankofa was a symbol of the official edifying histories of state, which sat in distinct contrast to the robust, earthy, Anansi-like rebellious impromptu narratives of the people. Asante history developed into a rich dialectical arena in which contentious debates could be waged by all kinds of people. While Mansa Musa had wrested the grander state and intellectual narratives from the griot, for the Asante, a nation born out of struggle and revolution, they would always be both Anansi, the irreverent spider, and Sankofa, the great narrative of state.

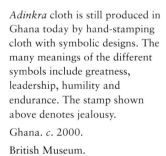

Adinkra cloth is still produced in Ghana today by hand-stamping cloth with symbolic designs. The many meanings of the different symbols include greatness, leadership, humility and endurance. The stamp shown above denotes jealousy.

Ghana. *c.* 2000.

British Museum.

The Asante found ways to embed the spirit of these important narratives within a variety of particular objects of value. This was done particularly successfully through *adinkra*, a system of visual aphorisms and potent visual icons, like Sankofa, that were carved, printed and built into the Asante material culture. These symbols elevated a variety of kinds of craft goods into vessels of narrative, but the very materials themselves could be invested with meaning. Cloth that could be worn, as stools could be sat upon, also became a convenient repository of history, a symbol of continuity. The Asante adopted adinkra-printed mourning cloth, decorated with block symbols of proverbial wisdom, as a way of physically and spiritually wrapping their loved ones in the stories and wisdom accreted over generations. The Asante embraced *kente*, a cloth traditionally woven in thin strips in a highly labour-intensive process, often made from the thread of unravelled European trade cloths. Kente was expensive and complex to make and so became synonymous with luxury, power and history. Unlike adinkra, which was often used as part of funerary tradition, kente was a cloth of celebration, status and wealth.

Where there was kente and the power it represented, there were also often drums. The Asante adopted drumming traditions that took

The two drums that form the *atumpan* set are tuned to different pitches so that they can 'speak'. They are primarily used to send messages from the Asantehene across the kingdom, to play welcome messages and recite praises during royal ceremonies, and to play Ayan (drum poetry).

advantage of the tonal nature of Twi, their mother tongue. The state drummers of the Asantehene (the king) would play the venerated royal drums on state occasions, reaffirming every audience member's connection to the state aurally, visually and intellectually, and casting an irresistible multimedia assault on the senses, designed to win citizens over to the narratives of state.

In its completeness it was a campaign to win hearts and minds unlike anything previously conceived in the region. Almost every area of cultural production was commandeered and refashioned to enhance and reinforce the status of the monarchy, the Asante state and the stool. The wealth, sophistication and ambition of the Asante set them apart from their neighbours and those that preceded them. It was success best demonstrated in the vast wealth of the state and how that wealth was skilfully utilised. Where Mansa Musa sought to use his wealth to build knowledge and accrue greater influence, Osei Tutu, steering his fledgling state through its early stages, sought voraciously, aggressively, to wrestle more power from his neighbours, to negotiate robustly for more territories with those who would accept his authority or to overrun the lands and cast the few that opposed him into slavery.

The Asante state was an insatiable machine that only understood uncompromising expansion. Osei Tutu's court seemed to enjoy that dominance, humiliating the vanquished and forcing those he conquered to pay gold tribute, and then regulating mining, refining

This sheet-brass box or *forowa* from northern Ghana is a rare rectangular version of a container often used for shea butter, but also for valuables including gold dust and cowrie shells. It is richly decorated with symbolic designs, including a stool, symbolic of kingship, and a spider, probably a representation of Anansi, the trickster character of West African and Caribbean stories.

Ghana. Collected *c*. 1900.

Pitt Rivers Museum, University of Oxford.

and distribution of the region's gold. That regulation was made most vivid in a system of centrally authenticated gold-weights, which like all great currency systems, beyond being a mechanism of exchange, served to remind citizens of what they owed the Asante state. Gold-weights could be representations of the magnificent court regalia and crown jewels, but they also captured regional stories and myths. They tied commerce to the state, not just in a system of tribute but more fundamentally through the stories of origin that all Asante shared.

By the time that Osei Bonsu, 'The Whale', ascended the Asante stool a century after Osei Tutu, the Asante territory stretched across much of what is today Ghana and Côte d'Ivoire. Even then, as a mature state, the Asante continued to be ruthless. They had acculturated a strategy of conquering neighbours and rivals, selling thousands into slavery or into the back-breaking work of clearing the forest, making arable land and driving and maintaining roads that radiated out from their capital to link isolated communities. They had created a political, topographical web of which the Asante court was the hub;

and if the spider, they were not as venomous as they once were, but they remained audacious in their aspirations and bold and uncompromising in the way that they carried out their plans. It is quite obvious why one of the great state symbols was Anansi, the impudent spider, and why the spider's web became a visual motif that adorned many of the great buildings and symbols of state. The Asante feared no one and when the taxmen travelled across the Asante countryside collecting tribute for the king, the gold flowed up the radials of the state web to replenish and enrich the stool at the heart of the empire.

Osei Bonsu enjoyed the title of 'The Whale' because during his reign, for the first time, the Asante took control of the coastal region, the long-coveted outlet for their gold and enslaved people. Thomas Edward Bowdich, Governor of the British settlements, captured something of this period in his seminal book *Mission from Cape Coast Castle to Ashantee* (1819).[5] The Asante court had become everything that the Asante founding fathers had hoped. And perhaps Osei Tutu's greatest aspiration of never being forgotten had been extravagantly

Thomas Edward Bowdich (c. 1791–1824) visited the Asante kingdom (in modern Ghana) in 1816 and was one of the negotiators of a peace treaty between the British and the Asante people. His observant and positive account of this visit includes this famous colour illustration of the 'yam festival', properly *odwira*, which illustrates the splendour and ceremony of Asante.

British Library 146.f.17.

achieved. Beyond the great symbols of state that had been instituted by its founding fathers, the Asante court now accommodated Muslim scholars and scribes and European travellers and tutors to augment the traditional linguists, historians and storytellers. At its heart was Osei Bonsu, the whale, or large pregnant spider, waiting, surveying his vast intricate web: a realm of intense intellectual exchange and scholarship, where his young princes were tutored and advised on the world beyond their territories.

In many ways this was the high tide mark for the Asante empire. It was a brief generation before enslavement was outlawed and the Asante economy began to fail, hamstrung by a lack of labour. Curiously, even after the Asante kingdom had ceased to be an unassailable force, the great narratives that the state had invested in, persisted. When, at the turn of the 20th century, the Asante monarchy were forced into exile by the British, it was the stool, kente cloth and the symbols of state that filled the vacuum and offered continuity. And for those sons and daughters of Asante who were so cruelly

واحتبى إلى الأكوار مركزًا جانبية
ويرتث إلى الأنوار مركزًا وجهة
وتشاهدت معنى لأبدا كشف سره
لقم أجبل الرئيسيات لذكرته
ومقلع تفسير الأفوثة فقيها
وأقفه رزق الله في المعالي حضرت
أفلبها وراحنو كذا كرته
أطوف بها جففا على طول المنية
أدرفطبا أفطبا الرزيد حقيقة
على أسابر الأقطا بأقول وترجمة
توسلبنا بكل كرر شدت
أمينك م الأشياء دهر يهتى

This is part of a devotional poem from a bound volume of manuscripts from Asante. The manuscripts consist mainly of amulets – written texts in Arabic conferring power and blessing. They illustrate widespread use of amulets and the importance of manuscript culture in Asante at this date.

Before 1875.

British Library OR 6559.

sold into slavery, who were forcibly carried away to new lives across the Atlantic, it was Asante drumming and Asante stories that would survive more defiantly than anything else. Today the stories of Anansi are as much Caribbean and North American as they are Asante – and West African drumming rhythms, buried deep within the substructure of popular music, belong to the world. That voracious, irreverent love of life, that zest for freedom and knowledge that drove Anansi to challenge authority, was the very spirit that drove the creation of the Asante empire, and perhaps contributed to the acculturated fearless, indefatigable desire of enslaved people to keep their traditions alive.

Today as strident intellectual forces such as Ansar Dine grow popular in West Africa, it is that spirit of irreverent intellectual defiance, the spirit of the griot, that holds ancient traditions in good stead. When the medieval king Mansa Musa made Timbuktu his capital, he looked upon his new city as the Medici family saw Renaissance Florence, as the centre of an open intellectual, entrepreneurial empire that thrived on great ideas wherever they came from. The city, the culture, the very intellectual DNA of this region is so beautifully complex and diverse that it will always remain in part located in story-telling traditions derived from the indigenous, pre-Islamic cultural traditions. The highly successful form of Islam that developed in Mali became popular because it accepted those freedoms and that inherent cultural diversity. And the celebration of that complexity, that love of rigorously contested discourse, that appreciation of the word, is the very spirit of Anansi, of West Africa.

Endnotes
1 François Rabelais, *The Complete Works of François Rabelais* (London: trans. Donald M. Frame, Berkeley: University of California Press, 1991), p. 40.
2 See D. T. Niane, *Sundiata: An Epic of Old Mali* (London: trans. G. D. Pickett, Longman, 2006) and John O Hunwick, *Timbuktu: Its Origin and Development after Islam Entered Africa* (Princeton, NJ: Wiener, 2007).
3 See Thomas A. Hale, *Griots and Griottes: Masters of Words and Music* (African Expressive Cultures, Bloomington: Indiana University Press, 2007).
4 Ivor Wilkes, *Asante in the Nineteenth Century: The Structure and Evolution of a Political Order* (Cambridge: Cambridge University Press, 1975).
5 Thomas Edward Bowdich, *Mission from Cape Coast Castle to Ashantee, with a Statistical Account of that Kingdom, and Geographical Notices of Other Parts of the Interior of Africa* (London: John Murray, 1819).

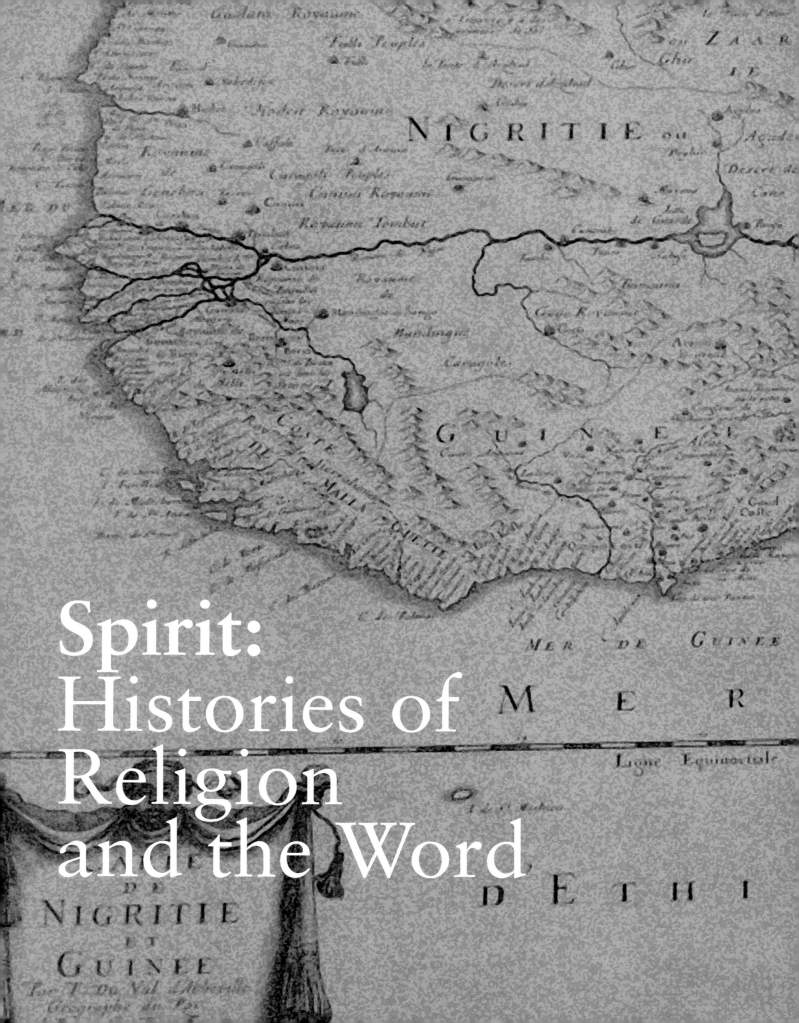

Spirit:
Histories of
Religion
and the Word

INSA NOLTE[1]

Manuscripts from West Africa were normally loose-leaf and kept in leather bags. The style of this illuminated Qur'an is typical of the region of southern Niger, northern Nigeria and Chad.
Late 18th/early 19th century.
British Library OR 16751.

All major forms of religious practice in West Africa – indigenous belief systems, Islam and Christianity – place a strong emphasis on the word. Capable of addressing both the profane and the spiritual, words are always potentially powerful links between seemingly mundane aspects of everyday life and the sacred. Words are not only used to transmit the information contained in oral and written texts, but they also serve as the practical means to transcend the boundaries between the past and the present, and between the secular and the divine. Through incantation, divination and prophecy as well as prayer, believers invest words with the power of communication with the spiritual world. The power of words to transcend the mundane is manifested in the transformation of the present, and of believers' lives.

Historically, indigenous belief systems have relied on a wide range of oral genres that were anchored by emblematic performances or in symbols. People used stories, songs, poetry, praise and prayer to appeal to a range of divine forces that would help them achieve success in the present, rather than promise a hereafter. Thus, while the spread of some practices was linked to the military successes and governments of West African states, others became popular through commerce and word of mouth. Spiritual forces that failed to respond to the needs and demands of their worshippers were abandoned in search of more promising ones.[2] As a result, the different oral genres associated with indigenous practices did not only educate believers about moral values and spiritual truths; understood as transcending the boundaries between present and past, secular and spiritual, words were experienced as powerful forces in their own right. In the predominantly oral context of traditional practice, their utterance confirmed the importance of human agency, power and reflection in the encounter with the divine.

Through their knowledge of Arabic, learned West African Muslims participated in the legal and scientific debates of the wider Islamic world and contributed to the documentation of local history and cultural practices. Yet while Arabic literacy had practical uses in transmitting knowledge across space and time, it was also the language of the revealed word of God in the Qur'an. This meant that

reading and writing were imbued with the capacity to link humans to the divine. As a result, Islamic practices based on the science of letters appealed to both Muslims and non-Muslims, and influenced the West African use of signs and symbols more generally.[3]

When predominantly Protestant Christian missionaries began to attract significant numbers of West African converts in the second half of the 19th century, they brought with them a different set of scriptures and practices. Unlike the Qur'an, the missionaries' Bible had no sacred language and could, after translation, be mass-produced in print. As colonialism and missionary education contributed to the wide spread of literacy, adherents of all religions engaged or re-engaged with the importance of the written word.

While some previously predominantly oral practices have been reduced to writing, the 20th century saw large-scale conversion to religions anchored in written texts, and while indigenous practices remain important in many parts of West Africa, most people became either Muslims or Christians. But the increased engagement with the texts of the Qur'an and the Bible has not meant that the spoken word has lost relevance. Today, the shared focus of both Muslims and Christians on praise and prayer confirms the spoken word as the most important form of communication with the divine.

Indigenous Belief Systems

West African indigenous belief systems were based on interactive and competing spiritual forces, including ancestors, deities, nature spirits and others, each one associated with a body of stories, songs and praise poetry as well as prayer. Ancestors, gods and other spiritual forces were not omniscient or omnipotent; they depended on the agency of humans for influence and recognition. Based on the assumption that once a deity has been empowered, it is in turn obliged to support its disciples, worshippers built up their gods through action, ritual and sacrifice, but also through words. Worshippers mastered the forms of speech and utterance associated with their deity in order to communicate successfully with the divine.

The human ability to access the divine was understood as rooted in human nature: both men and women existed in both the physical and the spiritual world. As each person arrived on Earth with her or his spiritual destiny, this could be discovered, actualised and changed through initiation and worship as well as through divination, prophecy and prayer. Names were an important part of this process. Some children might bear names that testified to the power of the deity that had rewarded their parents' prayers and requests. When spirit-children tormented their parents by dying young, only to be reincarnated again, they might be given special names that enticed them to stay in this world. Examples from the Yoruba include the names Dúrósinmí, meaning 'Stay [in this world long enough] to bury me' or Málọmọ́, 'Do not go again'. Treated well and addressed with these names on a regular basis, spirit-children could change their minds and decide to stay with their parents. Women were often particularly prolific in the use of poetry, proverbs, songs, chants and prayer to enlarge and popularise their deity.[4]

The ability of human agency to actualise the power of the word was also important in spiritual practices usually performed at the community level, such as masquerades. The beautiful Gẹ̀lẹ̀dẹ́ masquerades popular in southwest Nigeria and Benin ensure the fertility and general wellbeing of the community by encouraging women, and

A Gẹ̀lẹ̀dẹ́ mask decorated with talking drums.

Horniman Museum.

Some of the Gẹ̀lẹ̀dẹ́ masks provide social commentary and satire. This photograph was taken in 1970.

British Library Peggy Harper Collection C1074.

especially those among them who are feared to be witches, to use their powers in the service of the community rather than destructively. Dancing in many layers of multicoloured cloth while wearing distinctive wooden headpieces and metal anklets, the Gẹ̀lẹ̀dẹ́ masqueraders represent the communal ancestors who first performed this dance.[5]

Aimed at celebrating social harmony, the performance is not complete without songs which, drawing on the spiritual authority of the original Gẹ̀lẹ̀dẹ́ performers, comment on the moral state of the community. Bridging the gap between past and present and bringing the authority of spiritual beings to bear on everyday life, Gẹ̀lẹ̀dẹ́ masquerades address their audiences with explicit moral commentaries, and even social criticism. For example, Babatunde Lawal provides the Yoruba lyrics and translation of the song below, in which the singer exposes a member of the community who had brought stolen goods to him for safekeeping. Refusing to be involved in the crime, for which the offender has since been imprisoned, the singer celebrates both personal morality and the upholding of the moral order through the punishment of antisocial elements:

Akíyèsi o
Mo fẹ́ fi ẹjọ́ ọ̀rẹ́ mi kan sùn yín
Olórí burúku l' ọ̀rẹ́ mi
O ti mọ̀ pé ilé tí mo ngbé kò l'ẹ́hìnkùlé
Níbo lo fé kí i nf'ẹ́ran pamọ́ sí?
...
Ó dára, olórí burúkú, ọlọ́ṣà abèṣe,
À ṣé ogbà ẹ̀wọ̀n ni yàrá ẹ̀
Ẹní bá rí wọn ní Ìkòyí o
Ẹní j'orí ahun á sun kún.

Please, lend me your ears,
I want to report a friend of mine,
My friend is a bad-headed person.
He knows that my house has no backyard.
Where does he want me to hide a stolen goat?
...
It's all right, this bad-headed person, this thief and villain,
I did not realise that his bedroom was in the prison yard.
If you see them [prisoners sentenced to hard labor] at Ìkòyí,
Even the person who has eaten the head of a tortoise [the
    heartless] will be moved to tears.[6]

While the complex and shifting web of relationships between
humans and ancestors, deities and other spiritual forces did not reflect

Ifá divination.
British Library 4888.b.64.

a single hierarchical cosmology, it could nonetheless be understood as part of a greater system of belief. This is illustrated by the Ifá divination system. Associated mainly with the Yoruba of southwest Nigeria, Ifá, sometimes also known as Afá, is used widely in the area from southern Ghana to eastern Nigeria. Carried to Cuba, Trinidad and Brazil by knowledgeable enslaved people, Ifá is currently becoming increasingly popular in the United States. Based on the understanding that all events have roots and precedents in the past, Ifá offers guidance in the present by accessing a large oral corpus of stories, songs and riddles about different gods, spirits and cultural heroes, all of which are anchored in past divinations.

In order to access the texts relevant for the present, Ifá diviners use a divining chain or a set of palm or kola nuts, normally kept in a beautifully decorated bowl or cup, where they may also be washed with special substances. The chain or nuts may be thrown or passed between the hands in a particular way in order to produce two sets of patterns of eight marks each, called *odù* (an example is given below). The patterns are usually marked on a wooden divination board covered with special dust which helps to display the odù clearly. As there are two possibilities for each mark, marked with either one or two dots, there are sixteen odù; and the combination of two odù as the basis for a divination means that there are 256 possible configurations. Each of these configurations is linked to its own body of texts, and as many clients do not reveal the exact nature of their problem, the diviner often uses further odù to understand which particular section of this body of texts is appropriate for the situation. As all Ifá texts offer a clear recommendation of the action that was beneficent in the past, a successful divination session does not just offer its patron a story to explain her or his situation, but also practical advice on how to realise her or his ambitions.[7]

The size of the Ifá corpus alone means that it takes many years of learning and practice before a diviner is able to work independently. However, Ifá is more than simply a mechanical tracing of the text relevant for a particular problem. While there are scholarly, literary and religious collections of Ifá texts today, they cannot fully replace the diviner. Depending on the unique context of each consultation, a diviner emphasises the different voices, possibilities and disjunctures inherent in a particular text in different ways.[8] As individuals are empowered to understand their lives through stories, songs, proverbs and riddles located in the past, the recitation of Ifá texts does not simply offer their patron a chronology but enables her or him to realise deeper truths about life by transcending the boundaries between past and present.

Assuming the position of a mediator between human beings and spiritual forces, Ifá itself does not require exclusive worship, and its advice often includes suggestions about the deities and cults that

Geräte des Ifadienstes. Schalen zur Aufbewahrung der Ifakerne mit Schmuck von Tiergestalten und Ornamenten. Größen siehe Abbildungsverzeichnis.
(Gezeichnet von Carl Arriens.)

an individual patron should worship.[9] Ifá's ability to incorporate a wide number of competing, and sometimes contradictory, practices goes beyond indigenous belief systems. Structural similarities between Ifá and Islamic divination practices indicate that Ifá's current form was shaped by a close engagement with Islam.[10]

References to both Islam and, recently, Christianity appear in the Ifá corpus. However, the longer engagement of Ifá with Islam is reflected not only in the existence of several divinatory verses and stories referring to Islamic prayer, fast, dress and other practices, but also in the understanding that when the particular pattern called Odù Òtura Méjì, also known as Odù Ìmòle or Odù of Muslims, appears during the divination held for a newborn child, that child should be brought up as a Muslim. In some parts of West Africa, the original spread of Islam was closely linked to the revelation of such 'predestined' Muslims by Ifá.[11]

Odù Òtura Méjì

Yet while Ifá has incorporated Islam and Christianity into its own repertoire, the growing association of religious authority with a core text has meant that Ifá's oral nature is also considered a challenge by some of its adherents. Asserting that Ifá is a religious practice of the same order as Islam and Christianity, some of its followers have produced a Holy Book of Odù which they consider as a text that competes with the Bible and Qur'an.[12] Others argue that Ifá is not a religion that competes with Islam or Christianity but simply a way of revealing deeper truths that apply to all religions. This latter group includes many – though not all – West African Muslims and Christians who continue to feel that their religion does not prevent them from consulting Ifá.

Islam

As traders, scholars and advisers, Muslims played increasingly important roles in the West African empires of Ghana (*c.* 4th–13th century) from the 8th century. Between the 11th and 15th century, Islam expanded rapidly along West Africa's coast and the banks of its major rivers, and the ruling elites of Mali (*c.* 13th–15th century) and Songhai (*c.* 15th–16th century) as well as, further east, the Hausa states and Kanem-Borno empire (*c.* 9th–19th century) accepted Islam. As Islam became increasingly well established throughout West Africa, it played an important role in shaping West Africa's politics and its links to the wider Islamic world. At the same time, it introduced the systematic and formal engagement with the written word.

As the language of the Qur'an (the word of God revealed to the Prophet) and the ḥadīth (traditions of the Prophet) as well as other important texts, Arabic became West Africa's language of communication with the wider Islamic world. The Muslim geographer al-Bakri and the traveller Ibn Battuta produced early descriptions of West African societies (in 1068 and 1352 respectively). By the 14th century, West African scholars in centres of learning such as Timbuktu participated in wider scientific discourses on Islamic law, poetry and philosophy.[13] Islamic libraries throughout West Africa held work by authors from Morocco and Egypt, and West African scholarly training compared favourably to the education offered in centres of learning in those areas. In the 19th century, an independent West African Islamic scholarly tradition had begun to reproduce itself.[14] While high scholarly attainment was usually limited to men, women from clerical lineages sometimes also received a comprehensive education.

The spread of Arabic also inspired a creative engagement with other forms of writing. In medieval Mali, where Arabic coexisted with Berber or Tifinagh script, Arabic became the script in which writers

Page from a prayer book in Arabic, in the Hausa/ Kanem-Borno tradition of script and illumination.

c. 18th/19th century.

British Library OR 16924.

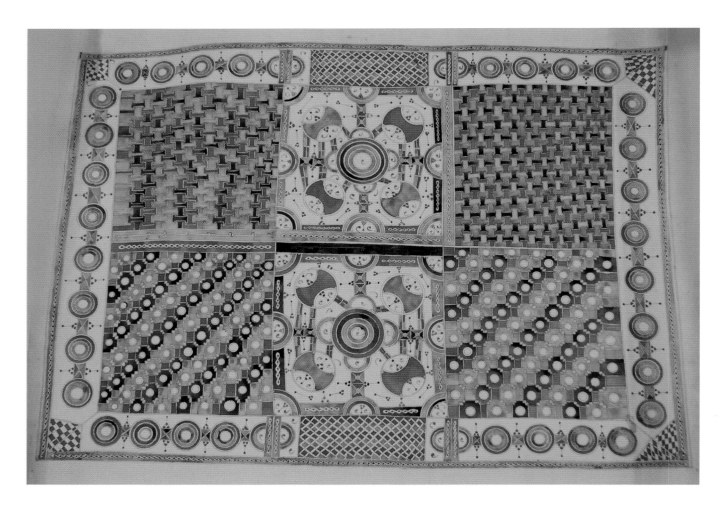

engaged with religion, legal argument and administrative and political communication. In contrast, Tifinagh was associated with the display of emotions, friendship and love.[15] Elsewhere, Arabic literacy inspired West Africans to transcribe and record their own languages for a variety of purposes, a form of literacy known as *ajami*. Ajami chronicles, myths and poetry were produced in many languages, including Wolof, Fulfulde, Bamanan and Hausa.

From the 17th century onwards the use of ajami increased as former clerics, often Fulbe speakers, established by religious war (*jihād*) a number of West African states, including Futa Jallon in modern Guinea, Futa Toro in present-day Senegal, Segu Tukulor in present-day Mali and the Sokoto Caliphate in what is today northern Nigeria. Ajami served as a powerful tool in the political mobilisation of Muslims not learned enough to understand the religious and moral arguments of the revolutionary leaders in Arabic. In the Sokoto Caliphate, Nana Asma'u (1793–1864), the daughter of its founder Usman dan Fodio, contributed to the political consolidation of the new state as the author of key historical, religious and other texts in Arabic and ajami.[16]

Pattern sheet showing manuscript illumination designs.
Northern Nigeria. 1909–34.
British Museum.

P.D. Boilat was one of the first three Senegalese to be ordained a Catholic priest. His *Senegalese Sketches*, published in 1853, is rich in portraits of a wide variety of people. This illustration shows a Muslim scholar writing an amulet for a widow (identified as such by her lack of jewellery). Boilat tells us that she is asking for a good harvest, and a better husband next time.
British Library 10096.h.9.

Even for Muslims with no or little access to literacy, Islamic practice emphasised the power of the word. The first two pillars of Islam, the declaration of faith in Allāh, the one true God,[17] together with the attestation of Muhammad as the Prophet of God, and the performance of five daily prayers, confirmed the importance of human speech in mediating relations between believers and God.[18] Obligatory prayers at dawn, noon, in the afternoon, at sunset, and

The use of wooden boards to learn the Qur'an in Arabic remains widespread across West Africa. Alexandra Huddleston photographed Qur'an boards, ink and pens in Timbuktu, Mali, in 2007.

British Library Photo 1294(6).

at night, were set apart from everyday life by ablution. Praising God and emphasising the believer's submission to His will, prayer enabled believers to engage in direct and daily communication with God.

The transformative power of the word is also illustrated by the fact that no initiation ritual was or is required for the conversion to Islam. Sometimes beautifully presented as calligraphic art, the declaration of faith alone, if said with conviction, is the means by which individuals become Muslims. Its words are simple:

لَا إِلَهَ إِلَّا اللهُ مُحَمَّدٌ رَسُولُ اللهِ

Lā ilāha illā-llāh Muḥammadun rasūlu Allāh
There is no God but God, Muhammad is the Messenger of God

As the word of God, the Qur'an was understood to be imbued with great power. In Qur'anic schools throughout West Africa, students' first major achievement was to learn to read, write and recite its complete text. Working through the book under the guidance of a teacher, students began by writing the first letter of the first verse of the Qur'an on a slate with locally made ink, learning how to pronounce it, and expanding their reading and writing skills as they worked their way through the complete text. It was only when they had completed their reading of the Qur'an, and knew the text by heart, that students were taught Arabic in order to understand what they already knew. In an environment where books were rare and expensive, the emphasis on rote learning and writing certainly contributed to the spread of the Qur'an. It also enabled enslaved West Africans to produce complete and partial copies of the Qur'an in the New World, and thus to retain their faith.[19]

The emphasis on reading, writing and recitation taught students the discipline and obedience that was required before they could begin to understand the words of the Qur'an. It also transformed them physically so that they would become suitable vessels for the word of God. Students memorised the holy text by writing it on slates or wooden boards. After the completion of a lesson the text was washed off carefully and the water containing the word of God was retained. Often, students drank this water, understood to be charged with the spiritual power of the text. In this way, a learned Muslim was transformed by the word physically, spiritually and intellectually. Religious knowledge and discourse depended, first of all, on self-mastery and transformation through the word of God. Learned Muslims not only knew the Qur'an's texts, they became living Qur'an themselves.[20]

Capable of addressing the widespread concern with health, wealth and general wellbeing, the power of the Qur'an also benefited less learned Muslims and even non-Muslims. Drawing on the power of the word, Islamic scholars prepared medicines and charms by producing medicinal water through the washing of slates or by

In West Africa, it was common for people to carry amulets written on paper, thought to give protective and other powers. Often these would be folded into a case of leather or sometimes basketry (as above, left) and worn as a necklace. The amulet on the left shows a 'magic square' and text from the Qur'an.

Top left:
The Gambia. Before 1869.
British Museum.

Left:
West Africa. Before 1963.
British Museum.

Above:
This lamellaphone contains an amulet repeating the two Arabic words for 'the Most Gracious, the Most Merciful', two of the 99 names of God.
?Guinea or Sierra Leone. *c.* 1898.
Horniman Museum.

copying relevant texts from the Qur'an onto amulets, cloth and other objects. Other ways of accessing the divine power of the word included divination and 'magic squares', which consisted of tables that contained numbers, or letters associated with numbers according to their position in the Arabic alphabet. These were believed to have divine properties and often added up to the symbolic equivalent of Allāh or the Prophet Muhammad. Through the reflection they engendered, such squares offered insight into deeper spiritual truths about God and creation.[21]

Ensuring the presence of the divine in the lives of believers, Islamic writing was much more than a technique involving the reduction of words to writing: it was itself a spiritual practice. Imbued with powerful symbolic meaning, the Islamic arts associated with writing were used in the decoration of everyday objects as well as in Islamic architecture in order to ensure divine help or blessing.[22] In many West African societies, non-Muslim symbols and artwork were inspired both by the visual beauty and the spiritual nature of Islamic letters.

For all Africans, but perhaps especially for Muslims, the establishment of colonial rule from the late 19th century was a moment of dramatic change. Even in places where the colonial state supported and integrated the existing Islamic aristocracy and protected Muslim areas from large-scale missionary influx, as for example in northern Nigeria, the widespread subordination of divinely sanctioned forms of authority to ostensibly secular laws and institutions led to fears and sometimes to conflict. Equally importantly, the fact that all colonial states relied on the languages of the colonisers meant that literacy in Arabic lost much of its importance as a political and administrative asset. But as improved infrastructure and security drew many groups of people into wider networks of exchange, colonial rule nonetheless saw a large-scale conversion to Islam in many parts of West Africa.[23]

The rise of Reformist Islam has transformed the Muslim engagement with the word across West Africa. Many Muslims attend secular schools in addition to traditional Qur'anic schools. In addition, the establishment of modern Islamic schools has benefited especially the education of girls.[24] Reformist Islamic leaders have also challenged the legitimacy of some of the practices that draw on the spiritual powers of the Qur'an and its scripts, such as the washing of Qur'an verses, which in turn is linked to the physical transformation and discipline of believers. At the same time, the translation of the Qur'an into local languages, and the increased availability of other non-Arabic religious material in print and other media, has enabled Muslims who are not literate in Arabic to understand the holy text.

Yet despite the growing production of printed religious texts, new forms of Islamic literacy have emerged in close connection with the oral. Given that only the Arabic text of the Qur'an is sacred, prayer books and Qur'ans for those not literate in Arabic also usually include a transliteration of the original texts. Enabling even readers with very little religious training to praise God and pray in exactly the same words originally revealed to the Prophet Muhammad, such publications confirm the divine potency of the spoken word.

Christianity

In most parts of West Africa, Africans first came into contact with Christianity during the transatlantic slave trade. It was, however, the end of the slave trade and the beginning of colonial expansion that opened West Africa to Christianity. The education, both in the United Kingdom and in the Sierra Leonean capital Freetown, of those liberated from enslavement played an important role in producing an indigenous West African Christian elite in the latter half of the 19th century. Many of these early Christian converts became successful proselytisers and church leaders in their own right.

Samuel Ajayi Crowther *c.* (1807–1891), the Head of the Anglican Church's Niger Mission, was born in Nigeria and captured by slave raiders as a young boy. Liberated by the British Royal Navy, he converted to Christianity and attended school in London and at Fourah Bay College in Freetown, Sierra Leone, before being ordained. From the 1840s onwards he was involved in a series of missionary enterprises in what is today Nigeria. In addition to translating biblical and prayer texts into Yoruba, Crowther also produced dictionaries, grammars and primers for several African languages. In 1864, Samuel Ajayi Crowther was ordained as the first African Bishop of the Anglican Church.

As Crowther's life illustrates, missionary work in West Africa was closely associated with the spread of literacy in the Roman script. Missionary endeavour was dominated by European Protestantism, which emphasised the importance of believers' being able to read the Bible for themselves. Working closely with African collaborators, missionaries studied and codified African languages in order to preach in local languages and to translate the Bible for African readers. As Christian missionaries relied on the printing press rather than on handwritten copies of their religious texts, they could offer a relatively stable supply of Bibles and religious books and pamphlets. The wealth of Christian print culture was admired and appreciated even in Muslim areas, although Muslim conversions to Christianity were relatively rare.[25]

The missionary emphasis on local language and literacy also contributed to the emergence of cultural nationalism. In written contributions to newspapers as well as pamphlets and books, literate Africans reflected on local culture and history.[26] Along the West African Coast, Carl Christian Reindorf and Samuel Johnson respec-

The Right Reverend Samuel Ajayi Crowther (*c.* 1807–1891), bishop and distinguished linguist, in 1861.

Lambeth Palace Library.

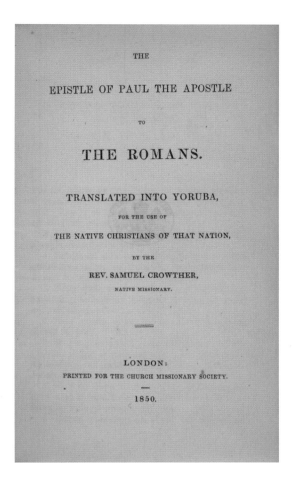

This 1850 edition of the Book of Romans, from the New Testament, is the first book of the Bible to be translated into Yoruba (a major language of Nigeria). Crowther, the translator, was the driving force behind the creation of the Yoruba Bible.

British Library 3070.c.7.

tively wrote *The History of the Gold Coast and Asante* (1895) and *The History of the Yorubas* (completed in 1897 but published in 1921), seminal political and cultural histories of the peoples to whom they belonged. This 'cultural work'[27] often contributed to the celebration and affirmation of ethnic identities.

As the demand for literacy increased after the establishment of colonial rule, missionaries also made an important contribution to the spread of European-type schools, which offered converts instruction in both secular and religious topics in colonial languages. While early Christian schools had paid parents to ensure their wards' attendance, by the 20th century Christian missions raised funds through school fees, and through the sale of notebooks and writing implements. The close association of Christianity with literacy in English and French, West Africa's most important colonial languages, privileged converts in their relationship to the colonial state. As newly literate Africans became clerks in the colonial administration or in European-owned businesses, they constituted the core of a predominantly urban intermediary class that produced and enjoyed new forms of popular art and entertainment.[28]

The fact that the Bible was translated into a wide range of West African languages, and that converts could learn to read it relatively quickly in their own (and colonial) languages, meant that the content of biblical texts was easily accessible to believers. This empowered African Christians to form their own conclusions about the practice of Christianity that had been passed on to them by European missionaries. Challenging the racist and European-centred policies of many missionary churches, churches founded by Africans in the early 20th century reconciled Christianity with important local practices such as polygamy by pointing to biblical precedents that legitimised them.[29] Biblical references to the importance of song and dance in worship, and the use of percussion instruments, also legitimised the use of African melodies, drumming and dancing in many churches.

Drawing on local understandings about the power of the word, West African Christians also challenged the emphasis of some mission churches on the metaphorical and symbolic truth of biblical texts. During West African revivals following the influenza epidemic of 1918 and during the 1930s, founders of West African Aládùúrà or 'prayer' churches emphasised the continuing nature of divine revelation based on biblical texts and promises. Many leaders of Aládùúrà churches asserted their communication with God through powerful dreams and prophecies. Their followers experienced the power of the spoken word when they successfully relied on prayer alone for their wealth, wellbeing and healing.[30] Aládùúrà churches often acknowledged women's particular access to the spiritual, and the Church of the Lord, founded in 1925, was one of the first churches in West Africa to ordain women.[31]

The spread of Christianity and mission-inspired literacy also contributed to the emergence of anti-colonial politics. Especially after West Africa was drawn into the economic and military struggles that accompanied the Second World War (1939–45), a growing number of Africans followed wider political debates, and eventually formulated ideas critical of colonial rule in the language of their colonisers. The example of the Catholic poet and philosopher Léopold Sédar Senghor (1906–2001), who became the first president of predominantly Muslim Senegal in 1960, illustrates the leading roles played by Christians during West Africa's independence years. Africa's emerging political leaders also co-opted Christianity in the service of their political ideals. Thus, Ghana's first Prime Minister, Kwame Nkrumah (1909–1972), famously drew on a well-known biblical verse[32] to urge his followers: 'Seek ye first the political kingdom and all else shall be added unto you'.

In recent decades, modern and globally orientated Pentecostal and Charismatic churches from West Africa have further contributed to the emphasis on the spoken word by encouraging oral practices that link the believer more closely to God and Jesus. In addition to encouraging believers to claim the blessings promised to them by God

Catherine Mulgrave-Zimmerman (*c.* 1820–1891) is seen here with her family. Probably born in Angola, she was captured as a child and placed on a slave ship to Cuba in 1833. She survived a shipwreck off the coast of Jamaica, where she was freed and became a mission teacher. In 1842 she moved to what is now Ghana, where she made a significant contribution to mission education. She married Johann Zimmerman, the head of the Basel Mission there.

Mission21, Basel.

This cloth was made for the Methodist Church of Ghana's Inaugural Conference in 1961.

British Museum.

through prayer and the repeated vocalisation of potent biblical or other passages, believers also confirm their relationship with the divine through their public testimony to Jesus' transformation of their lives. Believers who are filled by the Holy Spirit speak in tongues, that is, in words whose meaning is unknown to themselves, in the knowledge that these words will bring into their lives powerful miracles the exact nature of which is, at the time of their asking, known only to God. By emphasising the transformative power of oral practices such as prayer and testimony, many West African Christians affirm that biblical texts are not only moral and spiritual guidance, but also tools of communication with the divine.

The growing body of Christian literature remains, however, closely linked to the oral. The close engagement of West African Christians with the powers of the word has also given rise to a large volume of Christian print material advising believers on how to pray and to access the divine. By focusing on the different ways in which Christians need to relate to the divine as men and women, students and professionals, single and married people, and children and in-laws, such print material also contributes to the religious reformulation of a wide range of social practices and identities.

Conclusion

Although many West Africans have converted to Islam and Christianity during the 20th century, indigenous practices continue to play an important role in many communities. Often the histories of towns and villages are associated with spiritual forces, such as masquerades or divinations, that guarantee social harmony and which are directly or indirectly associated with the authority of traditional rulers or chiefs. While those facilitating the celebration of traditional festivals and the installation of traditional rulers and chiefs are often self-declared 'traditionalists', many Muslims and Christians participate in such festivals because they consider them to be part of their cultural heritage. But as a growing number of Muslims and Christians criticise participation in such events, it appears that the future of indigenous practices hinges partly on the words used to categorise them.

While religious conflict often involved indigenous practices in the past, it has been increasingly associated with religious competition between Islam and Christianity. In some parts of West Africa, Muslim–Christian conflict reflects the fact that members of different social or ethnic groups converted to different religions. As a result, religious difference is sometimes mobilised in contests over conflicting material interests. Drawing on the increased availability of religious texts and reflections in a wide range of local languages, Muslims and Christians have also contributed to conflict by criticising the practices and texts of the 'other' religion. But in many parts of West Africa, Muslims and Christians also live peacefully with each other, and even learn from each other. Beyond the ideological extremes, what matters to most believers is the power of religion to transform their lives. Even while they base their faith and practice on the written texts of the Bible and Qur'an, they continue to rely on the spoken word to actualise the promises contained within them.

Endnotes
1   The author gratefully acknowledges funding by the European Research Council (ERC) for a Starting Researcher Grant entitled 'Knowing Each Other: Everyday Religious Encounters, Social Identities and Tolerance in Southwest Nigeria' (Grant agreement no. 283466). She also thanks Paul Naylor for the Arabic text and transliteration of the Islamic declaration of faith. Finally, thanks to Muhammad Isa Waley for his perceptive comments on an earlier version of this text.

2   K. Noel Amherd and Insa Nolte, 'Religions (West Africa)' in D. Johnson, *et al.* (eds), *Historical Companion to Postcolonial Literatures* (Edinburgh: Edinburgh University Press, 2005), pp. 422–8.

3   Jack Goody, 'The Impact of Islamic Writing on the Oral Cultures of West Africa', *Cahiers d'Études Africaines*, vol. 11, cahier 43, 1971, pp. 455–66.

4   Karin Barber, 'How Man Makes God in West Africa: Yoruba Attitudes toward the Orisa', *Africa* 51 (3), 1981, pp. 724–45.

5   H. J. Drewal and M. T. Drewal, *Gelede. Art and Female Power among the Yoruba* (Bloomington: Indiana University Press, 1983).

6   Babatunde Lawal, *The Gèlèdé Spectacle: Art, Gender, and Social Harmony in an African Culture* (Seattle: University of Washington Press, 1996), pp. 132–3.

7   William R. Bascom, *Ifa Divination: Communication between Gods and Men in West Africa* (Bloomington: Indiana University Press, 1969); Wande Abimbola, *Ifa: An Exposition of Ifa Literary Corpus* (Ibadan: Oxford University Press, 1976).

8   K. Noel Amherd, *Reciting Ifá. Difference, Heterogeneity, and Identity* (Trenton, NJ: Africa World Press, 2010).

9   Bascom, *Ifa Divination*, pp. 11–12.

10   Louis Brenner, 'Muslim Divination and the History of Religion of Sub-Saharan Africa' in John Pemberton III (ed.), *Insight and Artistry in African Divination* (Washington and London: Smithsonian Institution Press, 2000), pp. 45–59.

11   Gbadebo Gbadamosi, '"Odu Imale": Islam in Ifa Divination and the Case of Predestined Muslims', *Journal of the Historical Society of Nigeria*, vol. 8, no. 4, 1977, pp. 77–93.

12   Karin Barber, 'Discursive Strategies in the Texts of Ifá and in the "Holy Book of Odù" of the African Church of Òrúnmìlà', in P.F. de Moraes Farias and K. Barber (eds), *Self-Assertion and Brokerage. Early Cultural Nationalism in West Africa* (Birmingham: Birmingham University African Studies Series, 1990), pp. 196–224.

13   J. F. P. Hopkins and N. Levtzion (eds), *Corpus of Early Arabic Sources for West African History* (Cambridge: Cambridge University Press, [1981] 2000).

14   Bruce S. Hall and Charles C. Stewart, 'The Historic "Core Curriculum" and the Book Market in Islamic West Africa', in Graziano Kraetli and Ghislaine Lydon (eds), *The Trans-Saharan Book Trade. Manuscript Culture, Arabic Literacy and Intellectual History in Muslim Africa* (Leiden: Brill, 2011), pp. 109–74.

15   P.F. de Moraes Farias, *Arabic Medieval Inscriptions from the Republic of Mali. Epigraphy, Chronicles, and Songhay-Tuãreg History* (New York: Oxford University Press for the British Academy, 2003).

16   Hamid Bobboyi, 'Ajami Literature and the Study of the Sokoto Caliphate', in Shamil Jeppie and Souleymane Bachir Diagne (eds), *The Meanings of Timbuktu* (Cape Town: Human Sciences Research Council of South Africa Press, 2008), pp. 123–33.

17   Like other Arabic words, Allāh is normally translated into English (as God) in this text.

18   The other three pillars are giving alms to the needy, fasting during the month of Ramadan and the pilgrimage to Mecca for those who are physically and financially able to perform it.

19   Rudolph T. Ware III, *The Walking Qur'an. Islamic Education, Embodied Knowledge, and History in West Africa* (Chapel Hill: University of Carolina Press, 2014), p. 69.

20   Ware, *The Walking Qur'an*.

21   Louis Brenner, 'A Living Library: Amadou Hampâté Bâ and the Oral Transmission of Islamic Religious Knowledge', *Islamic Africa*, vol. 1, no. 2, 2010, pp. 167–215.

22   Jean-Paul Bourdier, 'The Rural Mosques of Futa Toro', *African Arts*, vol. 26, no. 3, 1993, pp. 32–86.

23   Robert Launay and Benjamin Soares, 'The Formation of an "Islamic Sphere" in French Colonial West Africa', *Economy and Society*, vol. 28 (4), 1999, pp. 497–519.

24   Stefan Reichmuth, 'New Trends in Islamic Education in Nigeria: A Preliminary Account', *Die Welt des Islams*, New Series, vol. 29, no. 1/4, 1989, pp. 41–60.

25   Shobana Shankar, *Who Shall Enter Paradise? Christian Origins in Muslim Northern Nigeria, ca. 1890–1975* (Athens, OH: Ohio University Press, 2014).

26   Derek Peterson and Giacomo Macola, *Recasting the Past. History Writing and Political Work in Modern Africa* (Athens, OH: Ohio University Press, 2009).

27   J. D. Y. Peel, 'The Cultural Work of Yoruba Ethnogenesis', in Elizabeth Tonkin, Maryon McDonald and Malcolm Chapman (eds), *History and Ethnicity* (London: Routledge, 1989), pp. 198–215.

28   Karin Barber, 'Popular Arts in Africa', *African Studies Review*, vol. 30, no. 3, September 1987, pp. 1–78.

29   Elizabeth Isichei, *A History of Christianity in Africa: From Antiquity to the Present* (London: SPCK, 1995).

30   H. W. Turner, *History of an African Independent Church. The Church of the Lord (Aladura)* (Oxford: Clarendon Press, 1967); J. D. Y. Peel, *Aladura: A Religious Movement among the Yoruba* (London: Oxford University Press, 1968).

31   Deidre Helen Crumbley, *Spirit, Structure, and Flesh: Gender and Power in Yoruba African Instituted Churches* (Madison: University of Wisconsin Press, 2008).

32   The biblical verse is 'But seek ye first the kingdom of God, and his righteousness; and all these things shall be added unto you' (King James Bible, Matthew 6:33).

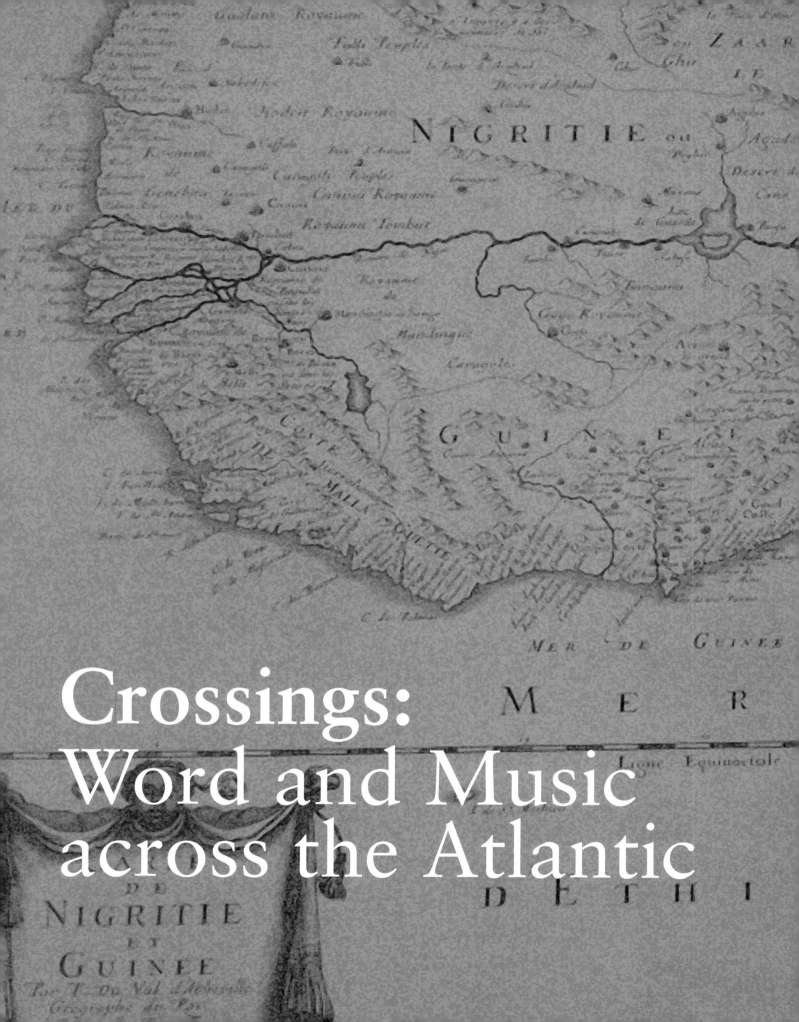

Crossings:
Word and Music
across the Atlantic

LUCY DURÁN, JANET TOPP FARGION
AND MARION WALLACE

Introduction

> Those people annually brought away from Guinea, are born as free, and are brought up with as great a predilection for their own country, freedom and liberty, as the sons and daughters of fair Britain.[1]

These words of the Black British writer Ottobah Cugoano (born *c.* 1757)[2] illustrate not only the inhumanity of the transatlantic slave trade, but also the enduring will to resist, to lay claim to their own humanity, of its victims and survivors. By 1800, the traffic in enslaved people from West Africa across the Atlantic had peaked: it is estimated that 50,000[3] were shipped each year and absorbed into a global system of forced labour. In all, from Africa as a whole and over the course of several centuries, it is thought that over 12 million people were enslaved and carried across the Atlantic.[4] There was, too, a longstanding and persistent slave trade northward across the Sahara, on a lesser scale – about 7,000 people per year by the late 18th century.[5]

The majority of those who survived the cruelties of the 'Middle Passage' across the Atlantic landed in the Caribbean and the Americas, where they faced both the back-breaking toil necessary to produce the sugar, cotton and other goods demanded by an expanding and industrialised world, and the systematic brutality required to keep such an extreme form of coerced labour functioning. Others, much fewer in number, ended up in Britain and Europe.

Wherever they found themselves, enslaved Africans both resisted the conditions to which their 'owners' subjected them, and profoundly transformed the societies in which they settled. In some areas of West Africa, there was joint and sometimes successful resistance to the depredations of slave raiders – often soldiers from states such as Asante and Dahomey, whose rulers sold people to the white traders occupying toeholds on the coast, such as the fort at Cape Coast Castle. Those captured and embarked on slave ships from the grim dungeons of castles such as these often tried to starve themselves or to jump overboard, accepting death as a fate preferable to enslavement.

Portrait of General Toussaint L'Ouverture, from the frontispiece to his *Memoires*, 1853.
British Library 10880.e.42.

This image of enslaved people cutting sugar cane is taken from a series of ten prints set in Antigua and published in London in 1823. It is based on a drawing by William Clark, an American traveller and artist. This picture presents a romanticised view, but it is nevertheless unusual in showing the labour carried out by enslaved people.

British Library 1786.c.9.

Once in the Caribbean and the Americas, enslaved people persistently and repeatedly rejected their subjugation, whether through individual acts of escape, disobedience and sabotage, attempts to improve their status, or collective rebellions which the ruling powers – though responding with the utmost ferocity – were ultimately unable to contain.

Enslaved people turned to creative expression to make alliances, assert themselves, and develop a sense of identity outside Africa. In this chapter we deal firstly with 18th-century Black writers to illustrate creative ways in which they used the written word in the cultures in which they found themselves, focusing particularly on writers of African origin in England. Using cultural theorist Stuart Hall's idea of 'routes and roots', the second section extends the range in time, space and genre to look at manifestations of spiritual and cultural experience and memory in the transatlantic context.

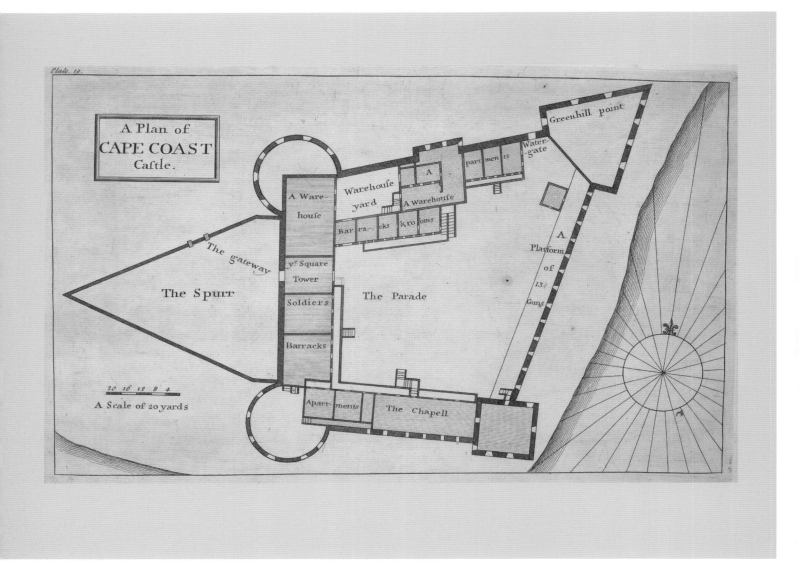

Plate 10.

A Plan of
CAPE COAST
Castle.

A Ware-
house

Warehouse
yard

A Warehouse

A
partments

Water-
gate

Greenhill point

Bar-ra-cks

Kro oms

The gateway

yͤ Square
Tower

Soldiers

Barracks

The Spurr

The Parade

A
Platform
of
13
Guns

20 16 12 8 4

A Scale of 20 yards

Apart-ments

The Chapell

Above:
From 1664, Cape Coast Castle
was the centre of the British
slave trade on the West African
coast, in what is now Ghana. Its
dungeons held captives until they
were forced onto slave ships.
This diagram from William
Smith, *Thirty Different Drafts of
Guinea*, 1740, was made as part
of a survey of forts for the Royal
Africa Company.

British Library 118.d.21.

Opposite:
This diagram illustrates how
captives were crammed into the
hold of the slave ship *Brookes*
– a real ship, plying between
Liverpool, West Africa and
the Caribbean – during the
transatlantic crossing. It is one of
the best-known images produced
by abolitionists in order to raise
public awareness about the
horrors of the Middle Passage.

British Library G.16302.

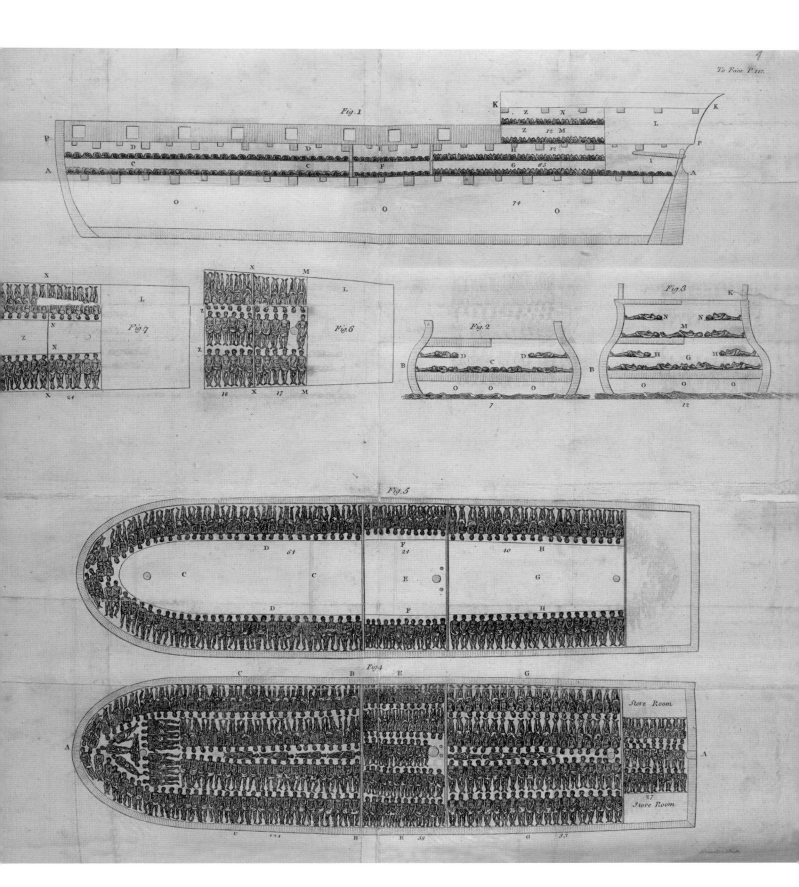

Instead of asking what are people's roots, we ought to think about what are their *routes*, the different points by which they have come to be now; they are, in a sense, the sum of those differences. ... These routes hold us in places, but what they don't do is hold us in the same place.[6]

Hall's words provide the perfect framework for an understanding of the creative relationships born out of the transatlantic slave trade, and especially of the power of music as an act of resistance, evoking and nurturing a sense of history and identity as musicians, genres and rhythms crossed and re-crossed the Atlantic.

Writing the Black Atlantic

In Britain and other European countries during the 18th century, Black writers, most possessing an intimate acquaintance with the humiliation of enslavement, fought against the system by organising politically and by the judicious wielding of their pens. It was in the last decades of that century, when the movement to end the slave trade was gaining huge momentum across Britain, that several outstanding African writers – including Olaudah Equiano (*c.* 1745–1797) and Phillis Wheatley (*c.* 1753–1784) – published books in England that would help to change how the British thought and felt about the practice of selling and owning human beings.[7] But half a century earlier, a Muslim nobleman liberated from enslavement had excited considerable interest in London and had succeeded in changing the policy of the Royal African Company (RAC) on who might be enslaved.

Ayuba Suleiman Diallo (*c.* 1702–?1773), known to the British as Job ben Solomon, was a cultured, high-status Muslim cleric from the state of Bondu, in modern Senegal.[8] In 1731 he travelled to the coast on behalf of his father to sell two enslaved people, but was himself, along with his servant, captured by rivals and sold to a slave trader destined for North America. Put to work on a farm, he was rescued through his own efforts and the advocacy of the clergyman Thomas Bluett, who escorted him to England early in 1733, where he was eventually to gain his freedom. In the following year he returned to Africa and subsequently to Bondu, where, to great rejoicing, he was eventually reunited with his family, although during his absence his father had died, and one of his two wives, believing him dead, had married again.

Diallo's story is an extraordinary one: the chances of returning after being enslaved and shipped across the ocean were vanishingly small. How did it happen? It is clear that his learning and piety as well as his natural authority were instrumental in bringing him to

An engraving made by Francesco Bartolozzi in 1796 from a drawing by John Gabriel Stedman, who fought against rebellions of the enslaved in the Dutch colony of Surinam in the 1770s. It shows one of the rebel fighters 'armed and on his guard'.

British Library 145.f.16.

the notice of the 'great and the good' in America and England. While in England, he scribed three copies of the Qur'an, which, like many learned Muslims, he knew by heart. He used his knowledge of Arabic to decode items in the collections of the Enlightenment scholar Hans Sloane, the founder of the British Museum and of its Library (today part of the British Library); and in 1734 he became a member of the Gentlemen's Society of Spalding, the earliest of England's learned societies outside London.

The height of Diallo's conquest of London society came with his presentation at court and the painting of his portrait by William Hoare. But London society was not, of course, entirely altruistic; and both Diallo and his patrons were enmeshed in the concerns and moralities of their own time. The RAC, which hosted and looked after Diallo in London (as well as 'owning' him for a time), was so concerned for his welfare because they saw in him a potential

Qur'an scribed by Ayuba Suleiman Diallo while in London, 1733.

Private Collection.

ally, a high-status African who offered, they hoped, an unparalleled opportunity to gain access to the African interior, and in particular to wrest control of the profitable trade in gum arabic from the French (efforts which ultimately came to nothing). Diallo himself, coming as he did from a hierarchical society in which enslavement occurred, did not denounce the practice in general. What he did manage to do, however, was to get the RAC's agreement to release enslaved Muslims (who could now be freed in exchange for two non-Muslims).

Jump forward half a century to an England with a Black population of perhaps between 5,000 and 10,000,[9] where the movement to abolish the slave trade was rapidly gaining momentum, and where a number of those formerly enslaved had managed to acquire an education and, in the words of Ottobah Cugoano, found reading and writing their 'recreation, pleasure, and delight'.[10] Cugoano, born in Africa in the mid-1750s, enslaved and brought to England, had attained his freedom by 1788 and worked as a servant in the house of Richard Cosway, the court painter. He is the most outspoken of the 18th-century authors of African descent on the subject of enslavement. In his *Thoughts and Sentiments on the Evil and Wicked Traffic of the Slavery and Commerce of the Human Species* (1787), he addressed the 'infamous and iniquitous traffic of stealing, kid-napping, buying, selling, and cruelly enslaving men' and called for the 'total abolition of slavery' and the 'universal emancipation of slaves'.[11]

Both Cugoano and his more famous friend Olaudah Equiano (also known as Gustavus Vassa) were important figures in the abolitionist movement at a crucial time. The Mansfield judgement of 1772, which ruled that an enslaved person could not be forcibly deported from the country, had effectively, if not explicitly, spelled the end of enslavement in England itself;[12] and while the British transatlantic slave trade was not banned until 1807, a mass campaign against that trade took off in the late 1780s. Equiano, Cugoano and many others of England's Black community – organising themselves as the 'Sons of Africa' – were actors in this campaign. They contributed by their writings, which not only put the case for abolition, but also, by the very fact that they existed, undermined the dehumanisation of the enslaved and demonstrated that Black people could not be equated with animals, as was common practice among the pro-slavery lobby. And they contributed by their actions, whether petitioning Parliament, or alerting activists such as Granville Sharp to injustices against enslaved people; the most infamous of these was the case of the slave ship the *Zong*, from whose deck, in 1781, the sailors threw 131 living Africans into the sea in order to conserve supplies of water for the crew and healthier captives on board.

Equiano was probably the most widely known and respected member of the Black population in the late 18th century. His book, *The Interesting Narrative of the Life of Olaudah Equiano, or Gustavus*

A portrait of Olaudah Equiano from the frontispiece to his autobiography *The Interesting Narrative of the Life of Olaudah Equiano, Or Gustavus Vassa, The African*, 1789.

British Library 615.d.8.

THOUGHTS AND SENTIMENTS

ON THE

EVIL AND WICKED TRAFFIC

OF THE

SLAVERY AND COMMERCE

OF THE

HUMAN SPECIES,

HUMBLY SUBMITTED TO

The INHABITANTS of GREAT-BRITAIN,

BY

OTTOBAH CUGOANO,
A NATIVE of AFRICA.

He that stealeth a man and selleth him, or maketh merchandize of him, or if he be found in his hand: then that thief shall die.
                                        LAW OF GOD.

LONDON:

PRINTED IN THE YEAR

M.DCC.LXXXVII.

Title page from Ottobah Cugoano, *Thoughts and Sentiments on the Evil and Wicked Traffic of Slavery*, 1787.

British Library 8156.b.22.

Vassa the African, Written by Himself (1789) tells the story of the author's capture in Africa, his experiences of enslavement, his struggle to free himself (which he achieved in 1766) and his many adventures at war and at sea, during his travels with the British navy. Equiano used *The Interesting Narrative* as a weapon in the campaign against the slave trade, partly through his skilful and tireless promotion and republication of the book – among other things he went on several speaking tours that doubled as abolitionist meetings – and partly through his descriptions of the horrors of the slave system. Here he is, for example, on sexual violence in the slave system:

> … it was almost a constant practice with our clerks, and other whites, to commit violent depredations on the chastity of the female slaves … I have even known them gratify their brutal passion with females not ten years old … And yet in Montserrat

I have seen a negro-man staked to the ground, and cut most shockingly, and then his ears cut off bit by bit, because he had been connected with a white woman who was a common prostitute ...[13]

In 1786 Equiano was briefly employed on the first scheme to establish a colony for freed slaves on the coast of Sierra Leone. Concerned about the numbers of the 'Black poor' in London at this juncture, leading abolitionists advocated a 'back to Africa' programme as a solution. Sierra Leone did eventually become a functioning colony and a refuge for those freed from enslavement, but not without its share of tragedy. Few of the first group of settlers survived the harsh conditions they encountered on the coast of Africa. In 1792 a new convoy set sail from Halifax, Nova Scotia, bringing 'Black loyalists' who had received their freedom as a result of backing the British in the American War of Independence. More successful in the long run, the new intake of settlers was nevertheless soon at loggerheads with the Sierra Leone Company; leaders such as Cato Perkins (d. 1805)

Above:
This print by Cornelius Apostool, produced in support of the abolistionist cause in about 1790, shows a colony of formerly enslaved Africans in Sierra Leone. It does not indicate the difficulties undergone by the first settlers, although the slave ship in the bay is a sombre reminder of the slave trade.
British Library Maps K.Top.117.100.

Opposite:
A portrait of the poet Phillis Wheatley, published in *Poems on Various Subjects*, 1773.
British Library 992.a.34.

and Isaac Anderson were able to use the written word to press home claims to the land they had been promised in petitions and letters that have survived in the British Library's collections.[14]

Another African author who had earlier put the publishing tour to good use was the poet Phillis Wheatley, who visited London in mid-1773 (when she was only about nineteen or twenty) to promote her *Poems on Various Subjects, Religious and Moral*, brought out by a London publisher in that year. Wheatley had been born in Africa, enslaved, and brought to Boston, Massachusetts, where her 'owners' recognised her extraordinary talent and made education available to her. Her poetry, widely applauded during her lifetime and noticed by Voltaire, addresses a wide range of subjects including the Christian faith to which she, like Equiano and Cugoano, wholeheartedly subscribed. Although her poems are not explicitly political, they have nevertheless been argued to contain coded references and new ways of seeing Africa:

> … And pleasing Gambia on my soul returns,
> With native grace in spring's luxuriant reign,
> Smiles the gay mead, and Eden blooms again,
> The various bower, the tuneful flowing stream,
> The soft retreats, the lovers golden dream,
> Her soil spontaneous, yields exhaustless stores …[15]

For Wheatley, divine purpose is at the heart of another work, 'On being brought from Africa to America', since the journey led to her conversion to Christianity. Nevertheless, this short poem ends with a ringing assertion of equality: 'Remember, *Christians*, *Negros*, black as *Cain*,/May be refin'd, and join th'angelic train.'[16]

Wheatley's standing as a writer and the stark contrast with her enslaved status were of concern to the other major British literary figure of African descent of this period, Ignatius Sancho (*c.* 1729–1780), who commented on the phenomenon of the poet's 'Genius in bondage' some time after she had left London.[17] Sancho is in many ways the most fascinating of the literary figures described here: born on a slave ship *c.* 1729, he attracted the patronage of the Duke of Montagu, who encouraged his intellectual curiosity and eventually employed him as a high-status servant in his household. Sancho was variously a prolific letter-writer – at that date letters were a recognised literary form, and Sancho's, which were published after his death,[18] form his main claim to enduring fame – composer, actor, art patron, family man and the owner of an independent grocery business (which, after his death in 1780, his son William converted into a publishing house). Sancho was also the only 18th-century Black Briton known to have voted in Parliamentary elections.

Sancho, urbane, sophisticated and often conservative in his

views, was nevertheless opposed to the slave trade, which he called 'the unchristian and most diabolical usage of my brother Negroes'. On reading a book on the subject, he declared that his 'heart was torn for the sufferings – which, for aught I know – some of my nearest kin might have undergone …'.[19] He also corresponded with Laurence Sterne, author of *Tristram Shandy*, praising his work and asking him to 'give half an hours attention to slavery (as it is at this day undergone in the West Indies …'. Sterne replied that he had, in fact, 'been writing a tender tale of the sorrows of a friendless poor negro-girl' and showing concern that 'so great a part [of the world], are and have been so long bound in chains of darkness and in Chains of Misery …'. The story of the 'poor negro-girl' forms part of volume nine of *Tristram Shandy*.[20]

Perhaps as significant as these writers' political struggles and views was the way in which they became part of the warp and weft of British, and indeed European and American, culture. As they struggled to make their mark in a world in which freedom itself could never be taken for granted, and in which the racism of the times exposed them to frequent ridicule and abuse simply for being who they were, the contribution made by these authors is truly remarkable. In the following century, new figures would emerge who also became

The title page of the fifth edition of *The Letters of the Late Ignatius Sancho, an African*, published in 1803 by his son William. This edition included an engraving taken from Thomas Gainsborough's 1768 portrait of Sancho.

British Library Add. 89077.

> Minuets Cotillons & Country Dances
> *for the*
> Violin, Mandolin, German Flute, &
> HARPSICHORD
> Composed by an African
> Most humbly Inscribed to his Grace
> HENRY DUKE of BUCCLEUGH, &c, &c, &c.
>
> London. Printed for the Author.

This collection of printed music, published in 1775, was composed by Ignatius Sancho during his time of service with the Duke of Buccleugh. The publisher uses the phrase 'composed by an African' to add a sense of the exotic and increase sales.

British Library H.1652.f.(31.).

part of European creative endeavour – people such as Alexandre Dumas (1802–1870), grandson of an enslaved woman and author of *The Three Musketeers*, and Samuel Coleridge-Taylor (1875–1912), composer of the massively popular *Hiawatha's Wedding Feast*.

By the end of the 18th century, abolitionist struggles were bearing fruit. Denmark ended its transatlantic slave trade in 1803, Britain in 1807 and France in 1818.[21] The cruelties of enslavement continued in the Caribbean and North and South America, however, and the institution itself would not effectively end in British territories until 1838; it continued in Brazil as late as 1888.

Final emancipation from enslavement came both from continued campaigning and the direct actions of the enslaved. Across the Caribbean, communities of the escaped established their independence, and in Jamaica such Maroon groups, led among others by the famous Queen Nanny, fought the British to a standstill and in the 1730s concluded formal peace with them. Memories of those experiences survive today in songs like 'Grandy Nanny' and 'Shedo', which tells the story of a Maroon woman who had to abandon her child while running from the British; the child, lost in the woods, was taught the song by a spirit and was thus found and reunited with his mother.[22] Toussaint L'Ouverture (1743–1803), who wrote in his memoir, 'I was a Slave, I dare to declare it', is famous for leading a successful rebellion in Haiti and becoming its governor.[23] The Jamaican rebellion of 1831–2, led by Samuel Sharpe (1801–1832), although put down with great brutality, also brought home to the planters and the British more generally the enormous cost of keeping the system running.

The achievement of emancipation was also, again, influenced by the literatures and stories of those who had experienced the system at first hand. Among them was Mary Prince (1788–1833), who after a life of extreme hardship in the Caribbean escaped from her 'owners' during a visit to London and dictated the story of her life, which became *The History of Mary Prince* (1831). Prince describes how she and her sisters were sold at market, placed 'in a row against a large house, with our backs to the wall and our arms folded across our breasts … our mother stood beside, crying over us. My heart throbbed with grief and terror …'. The girls were 'surrounded by strange men, who examined and handled me in the same manner that a butcher would a calf or a lamb …'.[24] The book, which became a flagship text of the campaign to abolish the slave system itself, goes on to describe the many other atrocities suffered by the author in a system in which 'mothers could only weep and mourn over their children, they could not save them from cruel masters – from the whip, the rope, and the cow-skin'.[25]

Illustration from James Mursell Phillippo, *Jamaica: Its Past and Present State*, 1843, depicting celebrations of emancipation in 1838. The picture shows several banners, carrying slogans such as 'We are free!' and 'Thy chains are broken, Africa is free!'.

British Library B.42.d.24.

Routes, Roots and Roundtrips: Musical Crossings over the Atlantic

Those who acquired an education and published their own accounts were, of course, a very small minority among the millions who survived the Middle Passage and crossed the Atlantic. But the cultures of Africa also survived – whether remembered directly or created anew in changed circumstances – and became vital in the struggle for daily and psychological survival. There are hints of how this may have happened in an account of the voyage of the slave ship *Hudibras* in 1786–7:

> In the death of the first slave, the females suffered a severe loss; she was the soul of sociality, and, amongst her countrywomen, an oracle of literature … When living, in order to render more easy the hours of her sisters in exile, she would sing slow airs, of a pathetic nature, and recite such pieces as moved the passions; exciting joy or grief, pleasure or pain, as fancy or inclination led. The use of the quarter-deck was allowed the female slaves, during these recitations and airs; where they formed themselves into circles … This songstress was also an orator…[when] she delivered her orations … the other females joining in responses, or a kind of chorus, at the close of particular sentences. An air of solemnity ran through the whole, which, though I did not understand the speech, seldom failed to affect my mind, in such a manner as to cause me to shed tears of involuntary sympathy: reflection suggesting that they might be speaking of friends far distant, and of homes now no more.[26]

The death of this woman was shortly followed by a rebellion on board, caused in part by rumours that her body had been eaten by the crew.

This story, told by a boy of sixteen at the time of the voyage, suggests the cultural roots of the forms of dance, music, oral literatures and religion carried over from Africa and (re)created in the Caribbean and the Americas. These are powerful and important, whether appearing in words, in the form, say, of stories such as Ananse or songs and vocabularies appearing in new contexts; materially, in the re-creation of musical instruments and other cultural objects; or conceptually and musically – in, for instance, religious and musical traditions that have journeyed varied 'routes' through the centuries, and survive and thrive to the present day.

One such religious practice is *candomblé*, an African-Brazilian religion born out of enslaved Africans, primarily of Yoruba and Fon descent. The West African concept of *àsé*, a Yoruba word known as *axé* in Brazil, is reinvented and relived as candomblé in Salvador (Bahia) in northeastern Brazil.[27] Axé is an energy, a power

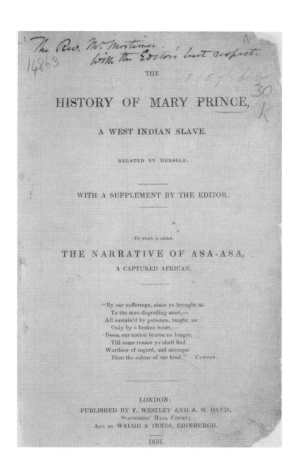

Mary Prince, *The History of Mary Prince, a West Indian slave*, 1831.
British Library 8157.bbb.30.

that individuals derive from their ancestral spirits, who are seen to act as their protectors. In religious contexts the candomblé practice involves spirit possession, thought to be brought about with the aid of singing, dancing and drumming, to connect with the spirit world. Candomblé influences all aspects of life, however, as the axé energy acquired assists people in reaching their potential and ambitions in a secular world too. Some practitioners also believe that the protection of axé is the force that has sustained Africans in many parts of the world from enslavement to independence and into the present day.[28]

In candomblé, and related religions elsewhere in what Paul Gilroy dubbed the 'black Atlantic',[29] we thus see the continuance of religious thought and worldview, spoken using West African words, performed using West African musical instruments and characteristics. Thus West Africa's *òrìsà* (ancestral spirit) becomes Brazil's *orixà*, Yorubaland's *sekere* (gourd rattle with cowrie shells or beads) becomes Brazil's *xequerê*, and the candomblé drums (*atabaque*) are played with the *agogo* (cowbell), a Yoruba word for bell.

The bell in most West African drumming ensembles holds everything together by executing a repeated rhythmic pattern known as a 'timeline'. This concept of time keeping is perhaps better known throughout the world as the Cuban *clave*.

Women dancing during candomblé rituals in Salvador da Bahia, Brazil.

This calabash bowl and lid are engraved with Nsibidi characters, used widely in south-eastern Nigeria.

Before 1911.

British Museum.

Indeed, many Cuban musical forms provide examples of Hall's routes and roots concept; the men's Abakuá mutual aid society is perhaps one of the clearest. The first Abakuá society was founded in Havana, Cuba, in 1836, its members mobilised to buy captives their freedom and participate in independence movements against the Spanish. Abakuá is derived primarily from the West African male secret societies (leopard or Ékpè societies) of the Ejagham, Efut and Éfik peoples of the Cross River region. In Abakuá ceremonies the actions of important ancestors from these peoples are enacted, recited and sung about. With the worldview came the secret Abakuá language. The language employs an ideographic form of script, known as *nsibidi* and primarily used to transmit symbolism in and among the Ékpè societies. While some symbols express communal ideas and are written on a variety of surfaces including walls and gourd calabashes, others are reserved only for society initiates. Such is the case in Abakuá, where practitioners adapted nsibidi to avoid the Spanish authorities.[30]

Abakuá has travelled a long and circuitous journey from the Cross River region in southeastern Nigeria to Cuba, where it was recreated by emancipated slaves in Havana as an all-male secret society believed to invest the members with power; then back via repatriated Cubans to West Africa – to Sierra Leone and to coastal Equatorial Guinea on the island of Bioko, where they encountered Éfik migrant workers and recreated Abakuá; and from there, transported with migrant Fang cocoa plantation workers well inland in that country where, known as 'Abakuya', it is today played for all festivities and is an important part of local Fang culture.[31]

Abakuá remains an active aspect of Cuban culture; its secret language and chants, having been (unusually) commercially recorded, its drummers sharing their talent, experience and knowledge of Abakuá beyond its confines and thus merging its influence into all major expressions of Cuban popular culture. The secret Abakuá language has influenced popular Cuban speech, appearing in common street language, and influencing Cuban Spanish. The worldwide penchant for Latin music has meant, therefore, that Abakuá influence, documented in virtually all forms of Cuban popular music since the 1920s to the present day on commercial recordings, may be felt throughout the world.[32] [33]

It is common knowledge that some of the best-known popular musics of the 20th century have their roots in Africa. The flow of African musical influences that led to the creation of such genres as calypso and steelpan (the mainstays of carnival), jazz, blues and salsa tends to be seen as a one-way trip: out of Africa into the New World. What is less known is that these musics have travelled back to the continent over more than two centuries, sometimes via circuitous routes, feeding into local traditions and generating new, exciting forms of music: Highlife, Rumba, Afrobeat, *gumbé* and so-called desert blues, to name but a few.

A closer look at what has been called the 'roundtrip' of African music points to a more complex trajectory than the description implies. These journeys have gone back and forth across the Atlantic, including to the United Kingdom, and have also zig-zagged around the African continent. They continue as new popular styles make their impact on both sides of the water, most recently with adaptations of reggae and rap by African artists. Meanwhile, African American musicians are increasingly immersed in the exploration of traditional styles and instruments from countries like Mali, where they search for the roots of the blues and jazz.[34]

A different but also complex international trajectory is evidenced in the music and practice of carnival. Caribbean carnival, the Mas tradition, began in the late 18th century with French plantation owners organising masquerades (*mas*) before the fasting period of Lent. Enslaved inhabitants, forbidden from taking part in carnival, devised their own celebrations called *Canboulay* (from

Calypso steel band drummers on float at Notting Hill Carnival, London, 2007.

the French *cannes brulées*, meaning burnt cane), which, in Trinidad and Tobago, became carnival.[35] With its calypso and steelpan music, arguably rooted in the West African griot (or other storytelling and social commentary songs) and percussion traditions respectively, carnival was brought to the United Kingdom from the late 1940s by new arrivals from the Caribbean. It has taken root in the UK, most famously in Leeds and in Notting Hill, London. Here we see the continuation of calypso – brought to the United Kingdom by calypsonians such as Lord Kitchener, and developed into newer forms, such as *soca*, epitomised by performers including David Rudder and many others – on platforms alongside other Caribbean forms of music including reggae and the sound system.

While there are many musical forms that could be used to illustrate Hall's concept of 'routes and roots', we will focus on two – *gumbé* and the blues – to highlight the impact of transatlantic musical crossings on the world's music and popular culture.

African gumbé is not widely known and is still under-researched, yet back in the 19th century it took West Africa by storm

Dancers at Notting Hill Carnival, London, *c*. 2000.

and was the first Caribbean style of music to go back to the continent, more than a century before recordings and radio facilitated the spread of music around the world. Its fruits can be heard today in some of Africa's most influential popular musics, such as Highlife and Rumba; while in the tiny West African country of Guinea-Bissau, it remains a powerful expression of national identity.

Gumbé / goombay / gumbay / gome, variant names for a drum and its music, began life in the 18th century on the island of Jamaica, among Maroon communities. We know little about its exact origins, except that it was the name for a large frame drum with four legs, built like a stool.[36] The classic drum of equatorial Africa is carved out of a single log and played with the hands. Such log drums were banned by slave owners in the Caribbean and southern United States, since they were believed to be able to 'talk' and communicate across long distances, rallying enslaved communities to uprisings.

The significant year of 'return' was 1800, after some 500 Maroons were deported from Jamaica to Nova Scotia in 1796 and from there in 1800 to the recently established Sierra Leone. Once on African soil, the Maroons introduced their music, gumbé, to the indigenous populations, and it was soon taken up by other repatriated freed slaves.

Sierra Leone became the point of dissemination for this Creole culture around West Africa: by the mid-19th century, communities of resettled slaves were established all along the coast in countries now known as Senegal and The Gambia, Guinea-Bissau, Ghana, Nigeria, Equatorial Guinea, and indeed as far south as Angola. Wherever they settled, gumbé went with them.

What defines gumbé as a style, and what accounted for its appeal in the 19th and early 20th century? One can only surmise as there are few references. The frame drum itself, the driving two-step rhythm (in contrast to most African traditions, which are in four beats with subdivisions of three) and the modern and perhaps risqué couple dancing were certainly novelties. But more importantly perhaps, since the music did not belong to any one ethnic or ritual context, it was a form of inter-ethnic entertainment in the new West African societies.

West African coastal people such as the Ga and the Kru played their roles in disseminating gumbé around West Africa. The Ga people, living around present-day Accra (Ghana's capital), travelled widely around the continent as labour migrants. One of their destinations in the early 20th century was the island of Bioko (Equatorial Guinea), with busy harbours and a flourishing trade where large numbers of Creoles from Sierra Leone were settled. The ethnomusicologist Barbara Hampton tells how Ga people working on Bioko picked up gumbé from Sierra Leoneans living there – as the Fang did Abakuá – and took the style back to Accra, where they called it gome, a music that responded well to the diverse population of the growing metropolis. There it influenced Highlife music.[37]

Highlife Giants of Africa: E.T. Mensah & Dr. Victor Olaiya – Highlife Souvenir Vol. 1, released in 1984. Mensah and Olaiya were acknowledged as the 'kings of highlife' in Ghana and Nigeria respectively.

The band Complex Sounds
performing at Talk of the Town
Hotel, Ghana in 1977.

A recording session with Desmali's group in Equatorial Guinea in 2013. Desmali comes from the island of Annobon. He plays the asiko square frame drum while his percussionist (on right) plays the gumbé drum.

Indeed, Highlife scholars like John Collins cite gumbé as one of the main foundations of West African popular music in the early 20th century. And London was buzzing with Ghanaian and Nigerian Highlife in the 1940s and 1950s. British music magazines such as *Melody Maker* had regular columns devoted to reviews of the Decca West Africa series[38] in the 1940s; the West African Rhythm Brothers, a Nigerian band led by Ambrose Campbell, were resident at the fashionable Abalabi Club in Soho, London, in the late 1950s. Their music was infused with gumbé rhythms. The Abalabi was a meeting place for musicians from all over the world, especially from Africa and the Caribbean, as well as jazz musicians from the United States. Such are the 'routes' that gumbé has travelled.

The country where gumbé remains the strongest as a living tradition is Guinea-Bissau, where it has been indigenised by musicians such as Manecas Costa (b. 1967). Here, gumbé became popular in the 1960s and 1970s as a statement of resistance to Portuguese colonial

Left:
An elderly African American man
playing a banjo, *c.* 1902.

Below:
The construction of the akonting
bears striking similarities to the
banjo of the American South. It
is an ancient instrument with a
long history although craftsmen
are still making them today.

rule. The Portuguese banned it from being played on radio, as they
did the Kriolu language that was the *lingua franca* of the many ethnic
groups of this small nation sandwiched between Senegal and Guinea.
Gumbé was used as a way of spreading information among guerrilla
fighters, and of calling for help from ancestral spirits. In some ways
this can be seen as a continuation of the spirit in which gumbé was
first created among Jamaican Maroons. Jean Rouch, the acclaimed
ethnographic film director, described gumbé as 'the dance of displaced
peoples and young revellers'.[39] It was also the sound of resistance to
colonial rule. Today it remains particularly strong wherever there are
Creole societies in West Africa.

The blues are probably one of the most influential and now
universal styles of American music, though their routes and roots are
far more obscure than those of gumbé. Their origins and development
in the southern plantations of the United States at the turn of the 20th
century have been well documented; and no one would deny that they

Ali Farka Touré, *c.* 1992.

have roots in Africa. Blues scholars cite the West African savannah belt, from Senegambia across the middle Niger valley in Mali down to northern Nigeria, as the most likely source. Such theories are hard to pinpoint without any written documentation, but the connection appears to hinge on two primary musical attributes: the preponderance of plucked lutes all across the savannah belt of West Africa – instruments such as the *ngoni, gambari* and *akonting* – that almost certainly influenced the banjo and later the use of the guitar as the core blues instrument; and the background blues riff against which lyrics and stories are sung, just as such musical templates in West Africa formed the basis of griots' praises and songs.

Ali Farka Touré (1939–2006), although from the Timbuktu region of Mali, was the first musician to adapt the repertoires and instrumental techniques of the north of Mali onto the guitar. His interpretations of Mali's desert music – using, for example, the non-standard tunings and finger-picking techniques borrowed from the gambari (oblong lute with skin sound-table) – tinged with echoes of the blues absorbed from albums he listened to in the 1970s and 1980s, have resulted in a whole new category of 'African blues' and 'desert blues'. When he first heard recordings of John Lee Hooker, he was astonished. 'I said, I don't understand this. Where did they come up with this culture? This is something that belongs to us'.[40] For Ali Farka, his 'desert blues' sound was merely reinforcing a connection that was already there and he always insisted his music was local and traditional. He was the inspiration for a whole generation of musicians, including the desert rock band Tinariwen and ngoni (lute) player Bassekou Kouyate (b. 1966).

The gambari and similar lutes played by griots from the middle Niger valley in present-day Mali provide one of the vital clues in the search for the roots of the blues. They are part of the direct ancestry of the banjo, an instrument that was first created as far back as the mid-17th century by enslaved peoples in the Caribbean, and later on in the southern United States from the mid-18th century onwards, then in Louisiana in the early 19th century. The significance of Louisiana was that many enslaved peoples were taken there in order to cultivate rice, bringing with them their own musical styles and repertoires. The Jola people from present-day Senegal, The Gambia and Guinea-Bissau were, among many other peoples such as the Bambara from the middle Niger, rice farmers forced into slavery, and who, with knowledge of their version of the lute, the akonting, also suggest a direct connection with the development of the banjo. The music of the slave banjo was certainly one element that contributed to the birth of the rural blues.[41]

For the most part, Ali Farka drew on the traditions of the peoples who lived in his desert region of northern Mali. Among his most cherished songs were 'Mbaudy', 'Poyi' and 'Njarou', which are more like templates, or basic accompaniments, than specific pieces – rather like the standard blues guitar that sits under most rural blues tunes. They date back to the precolonial era, and were originally sung by griots to encourage warriors before they went into battle. According to oral tradition, 'Poyi' was one of the last pieces played to war captives around Segu on the Niger, before they were either sold into slavery or beheaded.[42] Could the memory of this tune have stayed with captives sent across the Atlantic?

Thus we see stories of cultural retention and of adaptation and creativity in a wide variety of cultural forms: in religion, whose tenets came to pervade culture in the Americas as they did and continue to do in West Africa, and in music and literary forms emanating from the culture of crossings. The Atlantic region has been profoundly shaped by the movements of people from and back to West Africa; as individuals and communities, people brought their cultures, their world-views, their languages and their music, and employed them creatively as strategies for survival and renewal. African-inspired music has made the 'roundtrip' back to the continent, and been adapted, re-signified and reclaimed by local artists and audiences in a continuing process in which Africans on both sides of the Atlantic continue to identify with each other in a dialogue reconnecting people of African descent with their ancestral roots. A region woven together by these complex means has inspired expressive forms that, via the efforts of artists, musicians and writers and the force of historical events, have broken through into a much wider public consciousness, whether in 1780s 'must read' autobiographies and poems, or global forms of 21st-century music like the blues and Highlife.

Endnotes

1   Ottobah Cugoano, *Thoughts and Sentiments on the Evil and Wicked Traffic of the Slavery and Commerce of the Human Species* (London, 1787), p. 28. Republished as Ottobah Cugoano, *Thoughts and Sentiments on the Evils of Slavery and Other Writings*, ed. Vincent Carretta (New York: Penguin, 2007).

2   The date of Cugoano's death is unknown; it must have occurred in 1791 or thereafter.

3   Patrick Manning, 'Slavery and Slave Trade in West Africa, 1450–1650', in Emmanuel Kwaku Akyeampong, *Themes in West Africa's History* (Athens, OH: Ohio University Press, 2006), p. 109.

4   This figure is the result of major and sustained scholarly effort to estimate the actual numbers of those enslaved by using historical records. For more information see the Trans-Atlantic Slave Trade Database at http://www.slavevoyages.org/, accessed 27 March 2015. For a good general source on enslavement see http://www.understandingslavery.com/. For a strong collection of digitised images and discussion of their origin and meaning (particularly but not exclusively focused on the Americas) see http://hitchcock.itc.virginia.edu/Slavery/. For images of the Caribbean during the period of enslavement see the British Library's Caribbean Views at http://www.bl.uk/onlinegallery/onlineex/carviews/. All accessed 3 April 2015. There are many published histories of enslavement and the slave trade; the works of James Walvin are particularly useful as introductions to the field.

5   Manning, 'Slavery and Slave Trade', p. 100.

6   'A Conversation with Stuart Hall', *Journal of the International Institute* vol. 7 issue 1, Fall 1999, http://hdl.handle.net/2027/spo.4750978.0007.107

7   For a rich online guide to many of these authors see http://www.brycchancarey.com/index.htm, accessed 27 March 2015.

8   The fullest work on Diallo to date is Douglas Grant, *The Fortunate Slave: An Illustration of African Slavery in the Early Eighteenth Century* (London: Oxford University Press, 1968), which is based on extensive archival research although its language and conceptualisation is now somewhat dated.

9   This is James Walvin's estimate. James Walvin, *An African's Life: The Life and Times of Olaudah Equiano, 1745–1797* (London: Cassell, 1998), p. 132.

10 Cugoano, *Thoughts and Sentiments*, p. 12.

11 Cugoano, *Thoughts and Sentiments*, pp. 1, 130.

12 The judgement decreed that slave-owners could not forcibly deport enslaved people from the country: the latter could therefore not legally be sent back to the plantations in the Caribbean against their will.

13 Olaudah Equiano, *The Interesting Narrative and Other Writings*, ed. Vincent Carretta (London: Penguin, 2003), p. 104. Among many sources on Equiano see also Walvin, *An African's Life* and Vincent Carretta, *Equiano, the African: The Biography of a Self-made Man* (Athens, GA: University of Georgia Press, 2005); Arthur Torrington *et al.*, *Equiano: Enslavement, Resistance, Abolition* (Birmingham: Equiano Society, 2008).

14 For a brief introduction, and transcripts of correspondence by the Sierra Leone settlers, see Paul Edwards and David Dabydeen (eds), *Black Writers in Britain, 1760–1890* (Edinburgh: Edinburgh University Press, 1991), pp. 83–98.

15 'Phillis's Reply to the Answer', *Royal American Magazine*, January 1775, quoted in Phillis

Wheatley, *Complete Writings*, ed. Vincent Carretta (New York: Penguin, 2001), pp. 86–7. On aspects of Wheatley's writing (as well as the Black British writers quoted here) see also (for example) Vincent Carretta and Philip Gould (eds), *Genius in Bondage: Literature of the Early Black Atlantic* (Lexington: University Press of Kentucky, 2001).

16   Wheatley, *Complete Writings* (2001), p. 13. Emphasis original.

17   Sancho to Mr F., 27 January 1778, quoted in Edwards and Dabydeen (eds), *Black Writers in Britain*, pp. 27–8. Sancho did not appear to know that Wheatley had, in fact, obtained her freedom shortly after her visit. Carretta argues, with some plausibility, that Wheatley would have been aware of the Mansfield judgement and was probably able to demand her freedom in exchange for returning to America to look after her sick mistress. Carretta, 'Introduction' in Wheatley, *Complete Writings* (2001), pp. xxiii–xxvii.

18   Ignatius Sancho, *The Letters of the Late Ignatius Sancho … To which are prefixed, Memoirs of his life…*(London: J. Nichols, 1782). Republished as Ignatius Sancho, *Letters of the Late Ignatius Sancho, an African*, ed. Vincent Carretta (New York: Penguin, 1998).

19   Sancho to Mr F., 27 January 1778. Quoted in Edwards and Dabydeen (eds), *Black Writers in Britain*, pp. 27–8.

20   Sancho, *Letters* (1998), pp. 331–3.

21   Enslavement itself had been briefly abolished in French colonies after the French Revolution of 1789, but was later reinstated by Napoleon.

22   Kenneth Bilby, Notes to CD 'Drums of defiance: Maroon music from the earliest free Black communities of Jamaica' (Smithsonian/Folkway Recordings, 1992).

23   First published as François Dominique Toussaint L'Ouverture, *Mémoires du Général Toussaint L'Ouverture, écrits par lui-même, pouvant servir à l'histoire de sa vie …* (Paris: Saint-Denis, 1853). Republished as *The Memoir of General Toussaint Louverture*, trans. and ed. Philippe R. Girard (Oxford: Oxford University Press, 2014).

24   Quoted in Edwards and Dabydeen (eds), *Black Writers in Britain*, p. 158. For the full *History* see Mary Prince, *The History of Mary Prince: A West Indian Slave*, ed. Sara Salih (London: Penguin, 2000).

25   Quoted in Edwards and Dabydeen (eds), *Black Writers in Britain*, p. 164.

26   William Butterworth, *Three Years Adventures, of a Minor, in England, Africa, the West Indies, South-Carolina and Georgia* (Leeds: Edward Baines, [1823]), pp. 93–4. We are indebted for this reference to Shantelle George, '"King and Governor of all de Ebo people in Grenada"': Tracing the Igbo through Documentary and Cultural Evidence' (Paper to 3rd Annual Igbo Conference, School of Oriental and African Studies, University of London, 3 May 2014).

27   Axé has reinventions in other parts of the African diaspora – Vodou in Haiti and New Orleans, Santería in Cuba and Sàngó in Trinidad, for example.

28   Clarence Bernard Henry, *Let's Make Some Noise: Axé and the African Roots of Brazilian Popular Music* (Jackson: University Press of Mississippi, 2008) p. 25.

29   Paul Gilroy, *The Black Atlantic: Modernity and Double-Consciousness* (London: Verso, 1993).

30   See Ivor L. Miller, *Voice of the Leopard: African Secret Societies and Cuba*. Caribbean Studies Series. (Jackson: University Press of Mississippi, 2009).

31   *World Routes* on BBC Radio 3 at http://www.bbc.co.uk/programmes/b01shy5r.

32   Abakuá music has fed into Latin jazz, Cuban rumba and salsa. See also Ivor Miller, 'A Secret Society Goes Public: The Relationship between Abakua and Cuban Popular Culture', *African Studies Review*, vol. 43, no. 1, April 2000, pp. 161–88.

33   A major factor in the dissemination of this music back to Africa was His Master's Voice GV series, a catalogue of roughly 250 double-sided 78 rpm discs issued between 1933 and about 1958, specifically meant for the African market. Many West African musicians began their careers singing GV songs; Youssou N'Dour, for example, recorded 'Tu vera', a well-known Cuban *son* (composed by A. P. Echavorria) that was first recorded by the Trio Matamoros in 1928 and marketed in Africa by the Gramophone Company as part of the GV series. See 'Out of Cuba: Latin America takes Africa by storm' (Topic Records TSCD 927, 2005).

34   Such as Taj Mahal and John Lee Hooker, both of whom have collaborated with Mali's Ali Farka Touré.

35   See, for example, John Cowley, *Carnival, Canboulay and Calypso: Traditions in the Making* (Cambridge: Cambridge University Press, 1996).

36   It is probably a word of Bantu origin, related to other Caribbean musical terms such as *cumbia* (from Colombia) and *cucumbé* (from Mexico).

37   Barbara Hampton, 1979, 'A Revised Analytical Approach to Musical Processes in Urban Africa' in Kazadi wa-Mukuna (ed.), *African Urban Music*, special issue of *African Urban Studies*, 6, Winter 1979–1980, pp. 1–16.

38   See the British Library Sounds website at http://sounds.bl.uk/World-and-traditional-music/Decca-West-African-recordings.

39   Jean Rouch, *Ciné-Ethnography*, ed. and trans. by Steven Feld (Minneapolis: University of Minnesota Press, 2003), p. 167.

40   Martin Scorsese *The Blues*, part 1: 'Feel like going home' (Snapper SDVD0542, 2003).

41   See Gerhard Kubik, *Africa and the Blues* (Jackson: University Press of Mississippi, 1999) and Cecilia Conway, *Africa-banjo Echoes in Appalachia: A Study of Folk Tradition* (Knoxville: University of Tennessee Press, 1995).

42   Lucy Durán, 'POYI! Bamana Jeli Music, Mali and the Blues', *Journal of African Cultural Studies* 25:2, 2013, pp. 211–46.

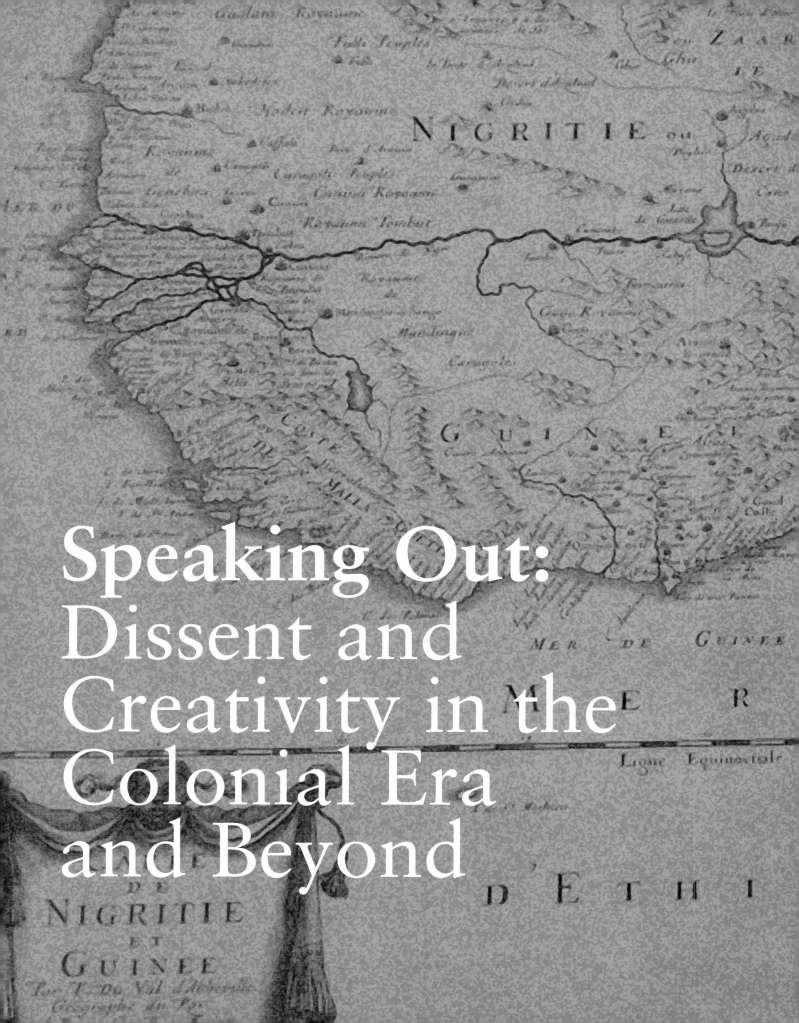

Speaking Out: Dissent and Creativity in the Colonial Era and Beyond

CHAPTER

FOUR

KARIN BARBER AND STEPHANIE NEWELL

The concept of authorship in West Africa is as vast as the region itself. An 'author' might be anybody from a Wolof-speaking oral historian in Senegal, for whom little is written down on paper and whose work is performed to music, to a university professor such as Wole Soyinka (b. 1934) from Nigeria, whose anglophone plays have been staged by elite theatres worldwide and whose work has been recognised in the form of a Nobel Prize for Literature.

West African literature encompasses a vast field of creativity, including the spoken word and dramatic performances as well as printed texts. Given such diversity, scholars often refer to West African literatures rather than using the singular form, literature. Familiar Western literary categories such as poetry, fiction, non-fiction and drama are not always appropriate to describe the creative outputs of West African authors, because the region's creative practices are enmeshed in traditions that are not necessarily compatible with them.

Literary activity in West Africa encompasses an enormous array of genres, styles and languages, including vernacular praise poetry,[1] funeral dirges, oral epics, oral religious and divination poetry, mythical and fictional narratives, lullabies, abuse songs, work songs, religious pamphlets, popular novels, printed autobiographies, hymns and testimonials, political protest poems written to be performed, self-help booklets, novels, poetry and plays. Each genre carries its own entanglement with the past and the present alongside distinct conceptions of authorship and audience. And, since the first printing presses started to produce material for African readers in the early 19th century, written literature has been produced in a wide range of languages, both African and European.

What, if anything, connects these linguistically and culturally diverse – some might say incompatible – art forms together? What, if anything, puts West African authors side by side in the same exhibition room? The answer involves far more than the identification of West Africa as a region on the world map.

Whether oral or written, performed or printed, West African literatures tend to be dynamic and socially responsive as well as creative and inventive. From the songs of oral performers to the tomes of history produced by early West African intellectuals and,

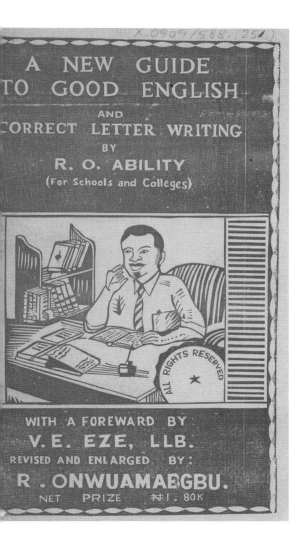

Front cover of R. O. Ability,
*A New Guide to Good English
and Correct Letter Writing*,
c. 1975.

British Library X.0909/588.(251.).

more recently, the morally instructive 'How-to' pamphlets published by local authors, many of the items on display in the British Library exhibition engage with the social and/or political debates of their times.[2] The first part of this chapter deals with literatures that not only described but also *participated* in protests against colonialism, and commentaries on post-colonial conflicts such as the Nigerian Civil War (1967–70). The second goes on to look at the rich variety of ways of 'speaking out' employed by West Africans in the public space, whether through word or symbol.

At its most extreme and deadly, the role of West African authors as participants in social and political debates is evidenced by the Nigerian government's execution of the creative writer and activist Ken Saro-Wiwa in 1995 for his role in the campaign for Ogoni civil rights in the oil-rich Delta region of Nigeria. Saro-Wiwa (1941–1995) was a public intellectual in a similar manner to many other West African authors, described below, including the revolutionary leader Amílcar Cabral (1924–1973) of Guinea-Bissau and the Cape Verde Islands, who was assassinated by the Portuguese for his anti-colonial views; both men, like the Nigerian poet Christopher Okigbo (1932–1967), were killed as a direct consequence of their political beliefs.

The Printing Press

In most of West Africa, printed books and newspapers were introduced through the intervention of Christian missionaries from the mid-19th century onwards; the process was accelerated and embedded by the establishment of colonial bureaucracy, after the entire region (with the exception of Liberia) was brought under French, British, Portuguese and German rule following the Berlin Conference of 1884–5. The Protestant missions in particular were committed to translating the Bible, hymn books and other devotional texts into local languages at the earliest opportunity, and distributing them in print as widely and rapidly as possible. Imparting literacy in local languages was a high priority, for they believed that the printed book could travel where the missionaries themselves could not, and could remain in people's houses quietly doing their work of edification. In many parts of West Africa where Christian missions were established, print and writing arrived simultaneously and in some West African languages the word for 'book' also meant 'letter', 'leaflet' and 'document'.

The missions also produced and published weekly or fortnightly newspapers; one of the earliest was the Church Missionary Society's *Iwe Irohin*, published in Yoruba in Abẹokuta from 1859 to 1867. The format and technology were quickly taken up by literate elites in major cities. In the late 19th century, an independent press flourished along coastal anglophone West Africa, linking politically and culturally active elites and fostering a climate of debate, criticism and reflection upon the transformations that West Africa was undergoing in the early stages of colonialism. This included African-language newspapers such as *Iwe Irohin Eko*, the independent Lagos paper published from 1888 to 1892. In the 20th century, the growth of colonial bureaucracy and the expansion of primary and secondary education meant that opportunities for self-expression through the written word expanded. Much of the literature thus produced was in English, but in some areas there was also an efflorescence of African-language written culture: Lagos, for instance, was the hub of a highly diverse and vigorous print culture in Yoruba that included histories, written poetry, novels, theological and philosophical disquisitions, moral homilies and documentation of local culture, and in the 1920s included five weekly newspapers. In Ghana, the leading nationalist J. B. Danquah (1895–1965) wrote in both English and Akuapem-Twi, and his vehemently anti-colonial compatriot Kobina Sekyi (1892–1956) wrote stories and plays in both English and Fante.

Print was often valued locally because of its assumed permanence and because it conferred authority. Early cultural nationalist elites embraced print as a way of simultaneously preserving and reforming knowledge hitherto transmitted orally. Print could fix things, and could record them for posterity as they happened. One of the purposes of print, as newspaper editors and book authors alike averred, was to capture the knowledge of the present for the benefit of future generations. In capturing it, they also edited and selected what they deemed worthy of preservation.

A large proportion of early printed literature revolved around the theme of West Africa's cultural history: authors spoke out against slavery in the mid-19th century and, in the early 20th century, they spoke out against colonial stereotypes of Africans as 'primitive', 'savage' and lacking distinctive cultural and political systems of their own. As the leading pan-African thinker and advocate of 'race consciousness' Edward W. Blyden (1832–1912) insisted in his many publications on the topic from the 1850s onwards, '[n]o nation or race has a monopoly of the channels which lead to the sources of divine grace or spiritual knowledge'.[3] Addressing a readership that stretched far beyond the colonial boundaries of West Africa, Blyden instructed Africans worldwide to 'bring themselves into touch with some of the general traditions and institutions of their ancestors, and … endeavour to conserve the characteristics of the race'.[4]

Whether through the newspaper or the book, printed literature returned again and again to the same theme in the first half of the 20th century. The humanism that underpinned the abolition of enslavement in the early 19th century was reiterated in the protest against European colonialism as authors emphasised the necessity to respect Africans' cultural differences from other social groups. Imperialism

Daguerrotype of Edward Wilmot Blyden (1832–1912), *c.* 1851.

and colonialism, as the man who was to become the first president of independent Ghana, Kwame Nkrumah (1909–1972), insisted, were 'unspeakably inhuman'.[5] 'We affirm the right of all colonial peoples to control their own destiny', he declared in a resolution adopted by the Pan-African Congress, held in Manchester in October 1945.[6]

One of the most sustained assertions of this theme can be found in *Ethiopia Unbound*, the philosophical novel by Joseph E. Casely-Hayford (1866–1930), with its revealingly non-fictional subtitle, 'Studies in Race Emancipation'. Published in London in 1911, *Ethiopia Unbound* portrays the life of a highly educated intellectual, Kwamankra, who probes European religious and legal questions from the standpoint of African spiritual systems.[7] Kwamankra's spiritual journey is a celebration of the subtlety and humanity of African society, over and against the raw polarities of the European racist belief systems that underpinned colonialism. In a parodic inversion of Rudyard Kipling's famous poem 'The White Man's Burden', colonialism and Christianity, and the lifestyles they bring to West Africa, are described in *Ethiopia Unbound* as 'The Black Man's Burden'.[8]

Casely-Hayford cleverly lays out his African argument by creating complex characters and a difficult literary text. In this manner, he offers literal – as well as literary – resistance to colonial ideas about the 'childlike' simplicity of Africans. Far more than a fictional exploration of one individual consciousness, the novel encompasses global African communities, including 'the Sons of Ethiopia the World Wide Over', as the dedication page states.

Authors such as Blyden and Casely-Hayford insisted that *all* humans are complex and culturally located, and that *all* societies have rich histories and traditions. From this standpoint, Blyden called on Britain 'to encourage the development of the natives along the lines of their own idiosyncrasies as revealed in their institutions'.[9] For Blyden and other Afrocentric thinkers, cultural differences should not be stamped out. Rather, they should be celebrated as a fundamental aspect of racial equality.

Such strongly race-conscious assertions of African difference characterise the literature of the first half of the 20th century in West Africa, and are summed up by the region's most famous novelist, Chinua Achebe (1930–2013), in his memoir: 'When the first Europeans came to Africa they knew very little of the history and complexity of the people and the continent. Some of that group persuaded themselves that Africa had no culture, no religion and no history'.[10]

In *Ethiopia Unbound*, Kwamankra resists these colonialist images of the cultureless 'native' by subverting their foundations: he is simultaneously witty, sarcastic, reserved, intelligent, sceptical and outspoken, as well as a natural leader who speaks impeccable English.

In this way, Casely-Hayford refuses to allow his African character to absorb the limited scope of others' beliefs and labels. When one reads *Ethiopia Unbound*, one is faced with far more than a novel: through this text, readers become immersed in the fields of history, politics, education, cultural studies and morality. Casely-Hayford brings his imagination to bear upon history and uses fiction to create a sense of future possibilities for West Africa, imagining a utopian time when Kwamankra's ideals will come to fruition.

For Nkrumah in Ghana, colonialism was 'the policy by which a foreign power binds territories to herself by political ties with the primary object of promoting her own economic advantage ... There are few people who would not rid themselves of such domination if they could'.[11] With the exception of Liberia, which had been granted independence in 1847, Ghana was the first country to achieve independence in West Africa, in 1957. It was followed by Guinea in 1958, the other French West African colonies (including Mali and Senegal) in 1960, the remaining British colonies (Nigeria, Sierra Leone and The Gambia) between 1960 and 1965, and the Portuguese territories of Cape Verde and Guinea-Bissau in 1973 and 1974 respectively. Independence was achieved partly through increasing militancy on the part of African elites and populations: the 1930s saw the rise of overt anti-colonial nationalist movements, labour unionisation, petitions, boycotts, strikes and riots. African-owned newspapers played a vital role in representing and mediating these events, providing opportunities for African leaders from across the political spectrum to interpret the spectacle of anti-colonial engagement.

The printing press was inextricable from Nkrumah's and other political leaders' anti-colonial movements in West Africa. Through their newspapers, books and pamphlets, these leaders spoke out on numerous topics including women's issues, African unity, socialism, farming, sport, French atomic testing in the Sahara, and apartheid in South Africa. As newspaper owners and editors, numerous key figures in West Africa read and cited one another's publications and participated in a transcontinental independence movement where African unity was the goal. Without the printing press, West African anti-colonial nationalists in the first half of the 20th century would have been ill-equipped to expand their power bases, to develop their trans-colonial political networks, or to gain recognition as political leaders.

On many occasions, local editors actively and vocally initiated political campaigns or participated in political movements. The Nigerian nationalist Nnamdi Azikiwe (1904–1996) was at the forefront of this anti-colonial activism. From his popular newspapers in the mid-1930s (the *African Morning Post* in Accra and the *West African Pilot* in Lagos) through to his leadership of Nigeria into decolonisation in the early 1960s, Azikiwe was dedicated to using

Kwame Nkrumah, the first President of independent Ghana, authored pamphlets, as well as books and newspaper articles, to put the case against colonialism. These illustrations from *How Dr. Nkrumah Conquered Colonialism*, 1954, testify to the wide appeal of his pamphlet *Towards Colonial Freedom*, first published in 1945.

British Library 08157.k.18.

An inspired reader of that powerful booklet.

the printing press to expose the unacceptable principles on which imperialism was built. His publications articulated his political vision for Nigeria, and continuously and confidently made declarations of anti-racism and anti-colonialism. He used the media as a platform from which he could call for a different kind of visibility for Africans to confront imperialist constructions.

At a time when the majority of Africans were denied political representation, newspapers thus furnished local authors with a vital forum for speaking out. Newspapers also provided space for experiments with creative writing, and many new writers found their first outlets in the press. Gladys May Casely-Hayford (1904–1950) contributed numerous poems to her father's newspaper, the *Gold Coast Leader*, in the 1920s. As one of the first writers to break away from Standard English in her poetry, she experimented with the syntax of Sierra Leonean Creole and successfully captured the nuanced voices of non-elite Africans in Freetown in her collection of poetry, *Take 'Um So*, published in 1948. She came from a highly literate, elite West African family that was inextricable from educational and literary developments throughout the region: while her father led early nationalist politics in Ghana and edited the *Leader*, her mother, Adelaide Casely-Hayford (1868–1960), was also a published writer, as well as a leading promoter of girls' education in Ghana and Sierra Leone.

Another talented woman writer, Mabel Dove (1905–1984), was a regular contributor to the newspapers. Her weekly 'Women's Corner', published in the *Times of West Africa* in the early 1930s under the pseudonym of Marjorie Mensah, carried witty commentaries on African elite society as well as occasional plays and serialised stories. Of particular note is Dove's parody of George Bernard Shaw's bestseller *The Adventures of the Black Girl in Her Search for God* (1932). Dove's version of the novella features a brilliantly sharp-witted African girl in a series of encounters with racist colonial men, patronising white missionaries and supercilious European women in West Africa. In a similar vein to her male counterparts on the West African press, after a long career in journalism, Dove went on to become an MP in newly independent Ghana.

Late 19th- and early 20th-century literature shows the impact of colonial labelling on African authors. Nearly all the key writers of the period describe how, in London or Paris, European eyes fall upon them with expressions of fear, disgust, fascination or desire. In *West Africa before Europe* (1905), E. W. Blyden wrote:

> During a visit to Blackpool many years ago I went with some hospitable friends to the Winter Garden where there were several wild animals on exhibition. I noticed that a nurse having two children with her, could not keep her eyes from the

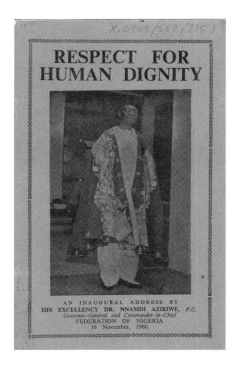

Nnamdi Azikiwe, *Respect for Human Dignity*, 1966. British Library X.0909/588(315).

Writer, educationalist and activist Adelaide Casely-Hayford.

spot where I stood, looking at first with a sort of suspicious, if not terrified curiosity. After a while she heard me speak to one of the gentlemen who were with me. Apparently surprised and reassured by this evidence of a genuine humanity, she called to the children who were interested in examining a leopard, 'Look, look there is a black man and he speaks English'. [...]

The unthinking European partly from superficial knowledge and partly from a profound belief not only in an absolute racial difference, but in his own absolute racial superiority, rushes to the conclusion that this difference of external appearance implies not only a physical difference, but an inferior mental or psychological constitution, and that the man possessing it must by assiduous culture by the European be brought up to the level of his teacher.[12]

By the 1940s, West African authors started to use creative writing to translate this trauma of misrecognition into social, political and artistic ideals. One particularly powerful reaction to the European gaze can be found in the poetry of Senegal's first president, Léopold Sédar Senghor (1906–2001). Senghor is famous for his artistic connection, in Paris in the 1930s and 1940s, with the Martiniquais poet Aimé Césaire (1913–2008) and other francophone African and Caribbean intellectuals, with whom he formulated the poetic movement known as Negritude. For the Negritude poets, touch, sound, taste and smell displaced the gaze from the scale of perception. Negritude poets reject the skin-deep visual economy of European racism and the supposed rationalism that accompanies the perceptions of white eyes. In their new existential economy, the other senses are brought to the fore, incorporating music, dance, song and noise.

'Prayer to the Masks' by Léopold Sédar Senghor

You who have painted this picture of my face over an altar of
    white paper
In your own image ... hear me!
Here dies the Africa of Empires – it is the agony of a ruined
    princess
And of Europe to whose navel we are bound.

Fix your immutable eyes on your children who are ordered
To give up their lives like the poor man his last vestment.
But let us now rejoice in the re-birth of the world
As it were the leaven needed by white flour!
Yet who would teach this new rhythm to a world wasted by
    machinery and gun?

Gold Coast's First Assembly Woman

Miss Dove won the Ga Rural seat for the C.P.P. at the General Elections in June. She is seen here watching the counting of the votes.

The entry of Miss Mabel Dove into the Gold Coast Assembly opens a new chapter in the political history of the country.

A new portrait of Miss Mabel Dove.

MISS MABEL DOVE, Member for the Ga Rural constituency, is the first woman to sit in the Gold Coast Legislative Assembly. She was elected in the General Election with an overwhelming majority, defeating Nii Amaa Ollenu, a prominent Accra barrister and Vice-Chairman of the Ghana Congress Party, and Mr. I. M. Peregrino-Brimah, a member of the Moslem Association Party.

Miss Dove is the daughter of the late Mr. Frans Dove, a Sierra Leonean lawyer domiciled in the Gold Coast, and Madam Eva Buckman of Accra. In her childhood she was sent to her two widowed aunts in Freetown, where she had most of her early education in her aunt's private school—Mr. Rice's School for Girls. She also spent a year in the C.M.S. (Annie Walsh Memorial) School. Later she went to the United Kingdom.

She returned to the Gold Coast and was employed as a shorthand-typist in a commercial firm in Accra. During this period she contributed articles to the "Times of West Africa", a local newspaper edited by Dr. J. B. Danquah, who was to become her husband. They had one child—a boy, now an undergraduate at the Gold Coast University College—but the marriage proved unsuccessful and there was a divorce.

Miss Mabel Dove, who, as the wife of a politician, was able to follow the trend of Gold Coast affairs, did not herself take an active part in politics until 1950 when Mr. Nkrumah declared "Positive Action" and was sent to prison. At that time she was a saleswoman in a commercial firm; she resigned and began contributing political articles to Mr. Nkrumah's paper, the "Accra Evening News". When Nkrumah was released from prison, he made her editor of the paper for a short period and since then she has been an active party member.

During the electioneering campaign there was a meeting of representatives from the Ga Rural Constituency of the C.P.P. at which she was introduced. Many of the representatives demurred, saying their local branches would find it difficult to support a woman candidate. Then one old man rose and told the gathering that they should remember that at one time in their lives each and everyone of them was dependent on the motherly cares of a woman, and that if Mr. Nkrumah selected a woman to represent them in the Assembly, he was, in fact, providing them with a "mother". She used that speech to advantage in the campaign.

Miss Mabel Dove has stated that apart from the needs of her constituents—water supplies, dispensaries, maternity clinics, roads, etc.—she would fight for women's rights. In particular, she would press for legislation to regulate customary marriage laws which prove ineffective against those men who marry "cloth ladies" (illiterates) only to send them away when they intend to marry "frock ladies" (literate girls). Whether she will be able to convince the 103 men she will meet in the Assembly only the future can tell.

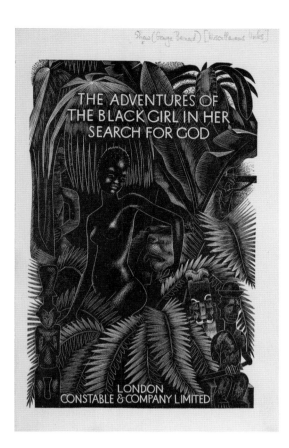

...

They call us cotton pickers, men of coffee and oil.
They call us the living dead.
We who are the men of the dance, and whose feet kick vigour
from the stony ground.[13]

This was not simply an experiment in poetry, or 'art for art's sake' in bohemian Paris. As with the long line of West African authors before and after him, Senghor insisted that '*la littérature et l'art négro-africains sont* engagés' ('African Negro literature and art are *engaged*').[14] Speaking out, for Senghor, was the first principle of African literature.

Whether situated in the early or later 20th century, any discussion of West African authorship needs to take account of international flows of culture and literature in and out of the region. No matter how 'local' in orientation, West African literature does not exist in isolation from other cultural influences. Many of the region's intellectuals were educated in Britain, France or the United States: they travelled the world, read one another's publications, and returned to West Africa with political ideas influenced by a wide range of race-conscious thinkers, including Booker T. Washington, W. E. B. DuBois and Marcus Garvey in the United States, as well as Karl Marx, Gandhi and the existential philosophers of 1940s Paris.

In West African territories controlled by the French and Portuguese, such as Senegal, Côte d'Ivoire, Guinea-Bissau and the Cape Verde Islands, Africans experienced a more centralised form of colonial rule than in British-controlled territories, where the policy of 'Indirect Rule' was designed to devolve government to local chieftaincies. French and Portuguese West African territories revolved around a policy of cultural assimilation whereby small elites were isolated from the population, taken to Europe to be educated and trained into leadership roles, and returned to the colonies as *evolués* or *assimilados*.[15] They were supposed to have literally 'evolved' into Europeans mentally and culturally.

The assertion of African cultural difference and pride became all the more urgent in this context. Amílcar Cabral, who led the anti-colonial struggle in Guinea-Bissau and the Cape Verde Islands, and was assassinated by the Portuguese in 1973, described the importance of African culture to the anti-colonial political struggle: 'the people are only able to create and develop the liberation movement because they keep their culture alive despite continual and organized repression of their cultural life and because they continue to resist culturally even when their politico-military resistance is destroyed'.[16] Over and against the deracinated evolués, he argued that 'over 99% of the indigenous population are untouched or almost untouched by the culture of the colonial power'.[17] These people were capable of

Amílcar Cabral, *Textos Políticos*, 1974.

British Library X.700/17009.

resistance. For leaders such as Cabral, the peasant masses in West Africa, with their rich heritage of oral genres, African languages and cultural traditions, form the cultural and creative 'source' to which the European-educated Africans must attempt to return.[18]

Popular Literature

From the earliest days of newspaper production in the 1880s through to recent popular literature, West African authors have taken on the mantle of opinion-makers and provokers of debate. Where newspapers provided a hub for literary activity in the colonial period, the late 20th century saw the emergence of DVDs and internet forums in which authors could circulate literary material.

Between the late 1940s and the 1960s, a period of intense nationalist activism across West Africa, a new generation of authors emerged: newly educated school leavers, mostly men, created new popular forms for their interpretations of the world. The most famous literature from this period was published in the large market town of Onitsha, in the Igbo-speaking area of eastern Nigeria. Known as 'Onitsha market literature', some of these anglophone pamphlets dealt with political and nationalist matters, while others contained advice and warnings, often about the untrustworthiness of good-time girls who 'pretend too much' and 'love only your money'.[19] These pamphlets contained templates for modern, urban living, with titles such as *Life Turns Man Up and Down* (N. O. Njoku), *Money Hard to Get but Easy to Spend* (J. C. Anorue), *How to Make Friends* (J. Abiakam) and *Never Trust All That Love You* (J. Abiakam).

One particularly popular plotline in these pamphlets depicts the rebellion of a young, educated woman against her illiterate

Below left:
Charles Uzoma Uwanaka, *Good Citizens, Good Country*, 1964.
British Library X.0909/588.(282.).

Below right:
Okenwa Olisah, *Life Turns Man Up And Down*, [?1964].
British Library X.0909/588.(158.).

father, who wishes to marry her off to an old chief for a hefty bride price. In Ogali A. Ogali's bestselling version of this story, *Veronica My Daughter* (1956), the heroine insists upon marrying the young man she loves rather than accepting her father's choice. Notably, in these pamphlets, the ignorance of the senior generation is represented by their blustering pidgin English: unlike the Creole community commemorated by Gladys May Casely-Hayford and the peasant masses celebrated by Cabral, fathers and elders are regarded as 'illiterates' rather than as founts of African oral wisdom in Onitsha market literature, set over and against the Standard English spoken by the progressive young heroes and heroines.

The Nigerian Civil War

The lively phenomenon of Onitsha market literature was halted by the outbreak of the Nigerian Civil War. On 15 January 1966 a high-ranking officer with an Eastern (Igbo) name, Chukwuma

Woodcut print entitled 'One of the bad effects of Nigeria Civil War –- "Kwasiokor"'. From Thomas Orlando Iguh, *Last Days of Biafra*, 1973.
British Library X.0909/588(290).

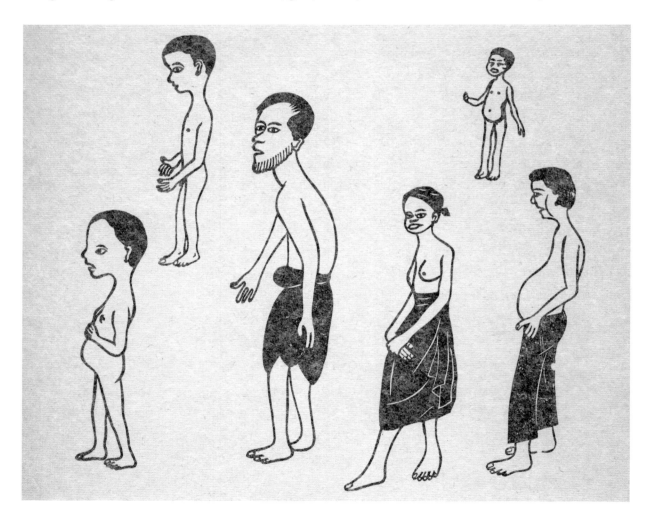

Nzeogwu (*c.* 1937–1967), led four senior army officials in a military coup against the civilian government.[20] They assassinated the prime minister, Ahmadu Bello, only to be crushed by Major-General Aguiyi-Ironsi, also an Igbo, who banned all political parties before himself being assassinated in July 1966. Two further generals and one failed political accord later, on 30 May 1967, leaders in the east of Nigeria severed ties with the Federal Republic. General Chukwuemeka Odumegwu Ojukwu (1933–2011) declared the eastern region the Republic of Biafra, and in response, with the support of Britain and the United States, Nigeria invaded Biafra on 6 July 1967.

Many printing presses and libraries in the east were destroyed in the war, and sanctions prevented the importation of paper for the production of newspapers and pamphlets, bringing the era of Onitsha market literature to an end. One of the few Onitsha publishers to emerge after the war, managed by the popular pamphleteer Nathan O. Njoku, was renamed Survival Book Shops as a testament to its resilience. In a poem entitled 'Lamentation', Azikiwe grieves for the loss of his library, containing 40,000 items and named after the anti-colonial nationalist and Nigerian intellectual Herbert Macaulay (1864–1946):

> My books,
> My most priced [sic] possession,
> Have vanished in the air.
>
> Warriors came,
> Blinded by spite and hate
> And destroyed my books.
>
> My books,
> My priceless jewels
> Nutrition of my soul.
>
> Dreary life
> Now confronts me,
> For my books are gone.[21]

The military coup that triggered the civil war was widely interpreted in Nigeria through the mesh of ethnicity as an Igbo push for power. What resulted from this interpretation of events was the massacre of tens of thousands of Igbos in the north of the country. Hundreds of thousands of Igbos were displaced to the east, where, according to the Red Cross, an estimated 1.5 million people died over the next three years of brutal violence, food-stoppages and starvation.

Among the dead was the poet Christopher Okigbo, who joined the Biafran army at the outbreak of the war and was killed in action three months later. Okigbo appears to have foreseen his own death

Christopher Okigbo, *Limits*, 1964. It was published by the Mbari Club, an association of writers, artists and musicians founded in Ibadan, Nigeria, in 1961.

British Library X.908/18811.

in one of his poems: 'If I don't learn to shut my mouth I'll soon go to hell,/I, Okigbo, town-crier, together with my iron bell'.[22] The survivors emerged from the war to speak out about their experiences: among them were the authors Chinua Achebe, Elechi Amadi, Flora Nwapa and Ken Saro-Wiwa, writing 'out of an experience red-hot with the memories and physical wounds of a most excruciating civil war'.[23] Indeed, so rapid was this literary response to the war that almost before the end of the conflict in January 1970, a new literary beginning could be identified in Nigeria as part of the 'the blossoming of the imagination which has followed in the wake of the war'.[24]

Written while the war was still underway, the first of these literary responses was *The Biafra-Nigeria War – A Human Tragedy* by Godfrey C. Okeke (1968). Books about the war were published in

WIVES AT WAR AND OTHER STORIES

BEWARE! WOMEN'S WAR IMMINENT

FLORA NWAPA

CIVIL WAR SOLILOQUIES

More Collection of Poems
By Nnamdi Azikiwe

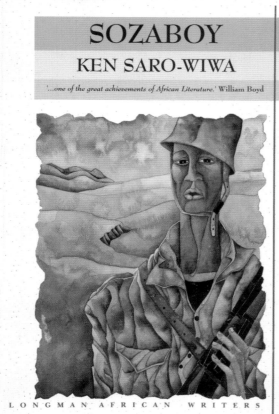

SOZABOY

KEN SARO-WIWA

'...one of the great achievements of African Literature.' William Boyd

LONGMAN AFRICAN WRITERS

ACADEMY AWARD NOMINEE
CHIWETEL EJIOFOR
AS
ODENIGBO

CHIWETEL EJIOFOR   THANDIE NEWTON
GENEVIEVE NNAJI AND ONYEKAONWENU

HALF OF A YELLOW SUN

DIVIDED BY WAR. UNITED BY LOVE.

IN CINEMAS APRIL 2014

rapid succession, from Elechi Amadi's *Sunset in Biafra: A Civil War Diary* (1973) to Flora Nwapa's unambiguously named memoir *Never Again* (1975).

As shown above, West African authors often address political, social and ethical issues through the medium of stories. In the decades since the end of the civil war, Nigerian authors have returned repeatedly to the trauma of what Nwapa referred to as a 'hell on earth'.[25]

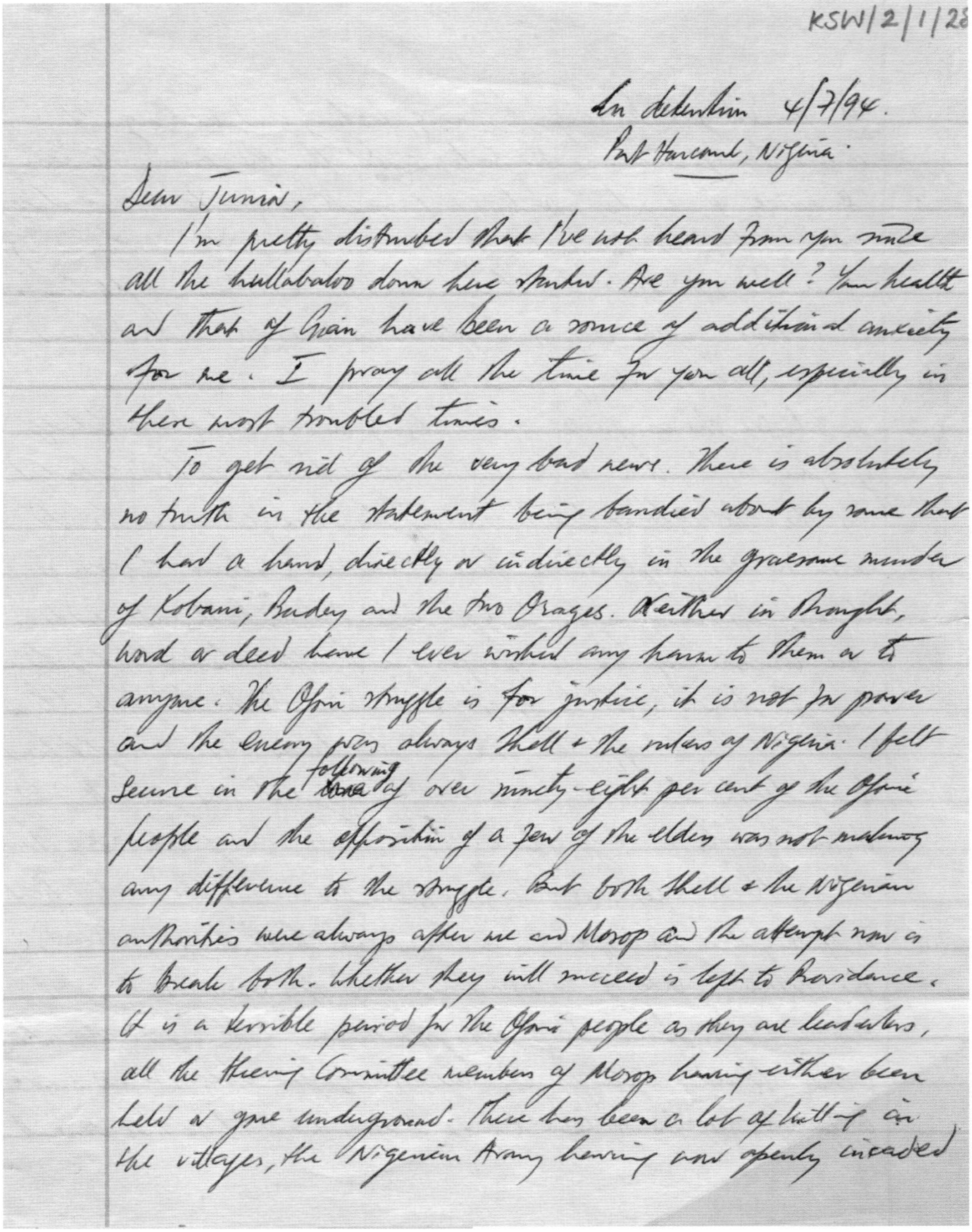

KSW/2/1/28

In detention 4/7/94.
Port Harcourt, Nigeria.

Dear Junior,

I'm pretty disturbed that I've not heard from you since all the hullabaloo down here started. Are you well? Your health and that of Gian have been a source of additional anxiety for me. I pray all the time for you all, especially in these most troubled times.

To get rid of the very bad news. There is absolutely no truth in the statement being bandied about by some that I had a hand, directly or indirectly in the gruesome murder of Kobani, Badey and the two Orages. Neither in thought, word or deed have I ever wished any harm to them or to anyone. The Ogoni struggle is for justice, it is not for power and the enemy was always Shell & the rulers of Nigeria. I felt secure in the ~~area~~ following of over ninety-eight per cent of the Ogoni people and the opposition of a few of the elders was not making any difference to the struggle. But both Shell & the Nigerian authorities were always after me and Mosop and the attempt now is to break both. Whether they will succeed is left to Providence. It is a terrible period for the Ogoni people as they are leaderless, all the Steering Committee members of Mosop having either been held or gone underground. There has been a lot of killing in the villages, the Nigerian Army having now openly invaded

The execution by the Nigerian government of the writer Ken Saro-Wiwa in November 1995 shocked the world. Saro-Wiwa, whose trial for alleged murder was widely criticised, had been a campaigner for the rights of the Ogoni people and against the devastating environmental effects of oil extraction in the Niger Delta region. In this letter, written from prison, he goes on to say, 'I'm at peace with myself, my conscience and my God… and I believe that the Ogoni and other oppressed minorities will secure justice in time as a result of the arguments I've made.'

Ken Saro-Wiwa to Ken Wiwa, 4 July 1994.

Ken Saro-Wiwa Jr and the Ken Saro-Wiwa Foundation.

In novels such as Buchi Emecheta's *Destination Biafra* (1982), Ken Saro-Wiwa's *Sozaboy: A Novel in Rotten English* (1985) and Chimamanda Ngozi Adiche's global bestseller *Half of a Yellow Sun* (2007), creative writers have inserted fictional characters into the bloody landscape of Biafra. In a similar manner to Casely-Hayford in the early 20th century, they intervene imaginatively in the recent past and use fiction to create alternative interpretations of what happened. Emecheta and Nwapa focus on the experience of women caught up in the war; anti-war writers, including Nwapa and Saro-Wiwa, deploy fiction to seek for 'humanity in a world gone mad'.[26] Other authors are more partisan. In his collection of poetry, *Civil War Soliloquies*, Azikiwe describes the leaders of the Nigerian government as 'scapegoats of history' and attempts to use poetry to reinvigorate a Nigerian national identity.[27] As recently as 2013, on the other hand, Achebe maintained a clear pro-Biafran perspective.[28]

Popular Word and Symbol

Though advanced literacy was associated with high social status – and remains so today – the written word was never the exclusive preserve of the elites, nor was it ever considered to be a domain sealed off from popular oral and musical mobilisations of the word. In West Africa today people wear cloth printed with names, slogans and proverbs. Taxis and mammy wagons (colourful buses and trucks transporting people and goods) bearing proverbs, nicknames and praise epithets colourfully inscribed on their sides ply the roads, with popular songs – often drawing on the same repertoire of verbal arts – blasting from their cassette players. Popular theatre companies in Ghana and Nigeria produce improvised oral plays with complex plots and rich verbal texts, sometimes based on oral narratives and sometimes drawn from printed literature. In the case of Yoruba popular travelling theatre, though the plays are orally improvised and change from day to day, the performers refer to an imagined script; and 'photoplay' magazines may convert such plays into a serialised photographic strip cartoon, thus re-scripting the oral performance. In all these ways, whether written, oral or symbolic, people speak out in public about the moral, social and political conditions of their lives, and about how the world could and should change.

Africa is known as the continent of the voice, with an unparalleled wealth of oral verbal arts that continue to flourish and evolve to the present today: songs, chants, stories and sayings connected with every social situation and event imaginable. This oral creativity should not be thought of as being in opposition to writing, visual inscription and print. On the contrary, inscription and orality have been intertwined as far back as their history can be reconstructed in

These 'fancy print' cloths are worn throughout Ghana. Cheaper than the more upmarket wax prints, they are generally imported into Ghana and given meanings in the Twi language by the market women who sell them.

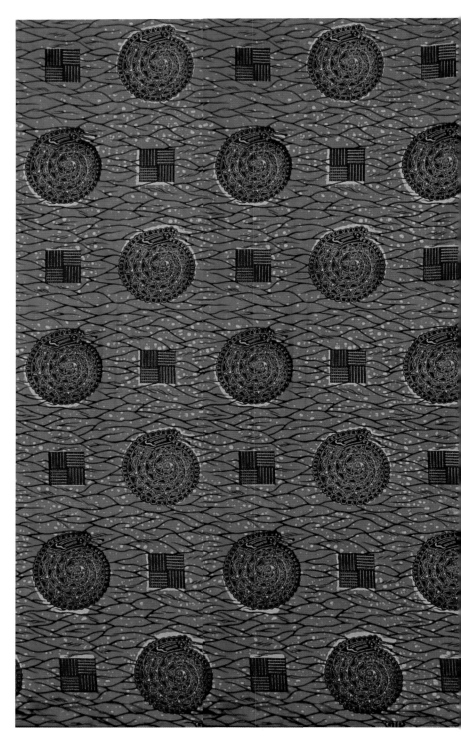

Opposite left:
'Your eyes can see, but your mouth cannot say' (some subjects are unsuitable for general discussion).

Opposite right:
'You treat me as if I were a snail' (indicating unhappiness in a relationship).

Right:
'Do not put your gold around the neck of a guinea fowl' (a warning to keep valuables safe).

An artist hand-painting designs on *Bogolanfini* cloth.

West Africa. People participating in an oral universe had a high regard for permanence, and for the transmission of verbal forms across time and space. Complex mnemonic cultures combining word and object were developed. Thus a proverb – being short, pithy and memorable – could be used as a trigger for a whole extended narrative. On hearing the proverb, listeners in the know would be able to expand it and tell the story that would 'explain' the proverb. One oral text led to another, each serving as a mnemonic for the next.

Oral creators also attached their texts to material objects. A particular tree or rock could serve as the starting point for a narrative that was associated with this landmark. In the Asante kingdom in Ghana, an elaborate material culture was developed which filled the social space with verbal texts: the finials on chiefs' ceremonial umbrellas embodied proverbs; gold-weights – small brass figures used to weigh gold dust in the extensive trading networks centred on the

Asante kingdom – were often designed to represent sayings or epithets relating to the owner; adinkra symbols, also evoking proverbs and other verbal formulations, were carved into wooden prestige objects and metal jewellery, and stamped on cloth. Across West Africa, cloth carried woven, dyed or appliquéd symbols that alluded to oral texts. In the indigo-dyed wrappers worn by high-status men in southeastern Nigeria, nsibidi signs were integral to the design and referenced important communal concerns. These ideographic symbols, of which nearly a thousand have been documented, formed a segmented mode of graphic communication, for while everyone seeing the cloth would be aware that it connoted high status, it was often only the maker of the cloth and a few of the highest rank in the men's association who would know the precise meaning.[29] *Bogolanfini* cloth in the Bamana-speaking area of Mali is woven, mud-dyed, and patterned with signs and symbols, which may refer to esoteric knowledge or may be combined to allude to everyday moral precepts.

Proverbs, in these cultural environments, were highly valued and productive of further text. They were nothing like the tediously sententious clichés they have come to be in Western cultures. Each proverb opened up into other proverbs, led to complex narratives or provided the ingredients of epics and praise poetry. Users were adept at interpreting them, giving them a new twist or countering one proverb with another. Since proverbs function as metaphors and only acquire full meaning in relation to the situation to which they are applied, each proverb is ambiguous and has the potential to mean many different things. Not only this, but people adept at creatively manipulating words and images would often create visual signs that could allude to more than one proverb. The viewer would be challenged to interpret it, and might come up with alternative 'readings'.

Thus the Asante gold-weight showing two leopards might call to mind several different proverbs: 'The rain wets the leopard's spots but does not wash them off'; 'when a leopard is hard pressed for food, it chews grass'; 'the leopard that prowls about under the thicket causes the thicket to shake greatly'; 'if the leopard could spring upon its prey to the right hand, then no animal would be left alive in the bush'; 'no one teaches a leopard's cub how to spring'; 'a hungry leopard tries to eat any animal'. And most proverbs can be interpreted in more than one way. For example, the gold-weight depicting two crocodiles with one stomach embodies the Asante proverb *Funtufunefu, dɛnkyɛmfunefu, won ɛfuru bom, nso woredidi a na woreko*, meaning that even though they have one stomach, they fight over food when eating. This proverb may be quoted to illustrate selfishness, when individuals within a collective enterprise start competing in an attempt to seize everything for themselves. But it can also be interpreted to signify the opposite. In a booklet about Asante adinkra symbols, this same image

This gold-weight shows two crocodiles with one stomach – a motif indicating competition or, depending on the interpretation, interdependence.

Ghana. 18th–20th century.

British Museum.

of the two-headed crocodile is interpreted to stand for a democratic process of governance where divergent views are expressed and people agree to disagree in order to arrive at a policy acceptable to all.[30] The participants in this culture were active interpreters of the signs and symbols displayed all around them.

By combining a number of objects with definite, accepted meanings, more complex and precise messages could be conveyed. Yoruba àrokò was a system of this kind. Secret messages, and messages to someone at a distance, could be sent by combining the objects and tying them up in a cloth so that the messenger who carried them, and bystanders along the way, would not see them. Such messages were held to have the advantage of being both succinct and undeniable: once sent, a statement conveyed by the objects could not be taken back as ordinary speech could. The objects remained as their own record. The objects' meanings often involved punning and word-play. For example, a piece of *èsúrú* (a kind of yam) stood for *sùúrù* (patience) because of the similarity in sound; an *òòyà* (comb) stood for a separation or break-up between lovers or friends, because *yà* means to part. Others were symbolic: two cowries bound together face to face, for example, meant that the sender wished the recipient, his true love, to come and see him as soon as possible. Others, again, referred to proverbs: a ripe, split cotton boll referred to the proverb 'The farm-owner is never angry that the cotton plants have split'. Combined with a strand of a newborn baby's hair, this message could be sent to a husband to tell him that his wife had safely given birth. The secure transmission of such messages depended on both participants knowing the code. Among the objects frequently used were particular types of stones, plants, tools, cloth and animal bones or skin.[31]

Messages conveyed by objects were paralleled by sonic patterns played on 'talking' drums and flutes, and even blacksmiths' anvils, which when struck with the hammer could be made to play tunes. The variations in pitch produced on these instruments represented tonal patterns in West African languages. Since several completely different sentences could have the same tonal pattern, interpreting sonic systems depended on listeners being familiar with the repertoire of sayings, greetings and praises that the performers were likely to play.

Thus 'writing' in the usual sense of the word did not enter West African oral cultures as a completely alien or unprecedented phenomenon. Practices of inscription through visual images and symbols, and the attachment of oral texts to material objects, were elaborate and widely known. Practices of interpretation involved production of further text – as when a gold-weight is explained by a proverb, which in turn is explained by a narrative, which in turn may contain further proverbs or poems. Practices of textual creation thus meant inhabiting a whole field of interconnected texts that could be traversed in different directions and by different routes, forming different constellations each time; and interpreting an oral text was as creative as composing one.

As discussed in the Introduction, writing in the conventional sense of the word was also known quite early in West Africa's history, in certain regions and among certain sections of the population. Among the Tuareg of the Sahel, the Tifinagh script was widely known at least 1,500 years ago; and in Mali, Arabic inscriptions on tombstones date back to as early as the 11th century CE. It was in the 19th and 20th century, however, that a new flurry of activity by local innovators in West Africa resulted in the invention of new scripts.

In Liberia in the early 19th century, the story goes that Mọmọlu Duwalu Bukẹlẹ had a dream in which a venerable white man showed him a book and taught him how to write the Vai words it contained.

Àrokò message of peace and goodwill sent by the King of Ijebu to the King of Lagos in 1851–2. (This is probably a copy of the original.) Collected before 1887.

Pitt Rivers Museum, University of Oxford.

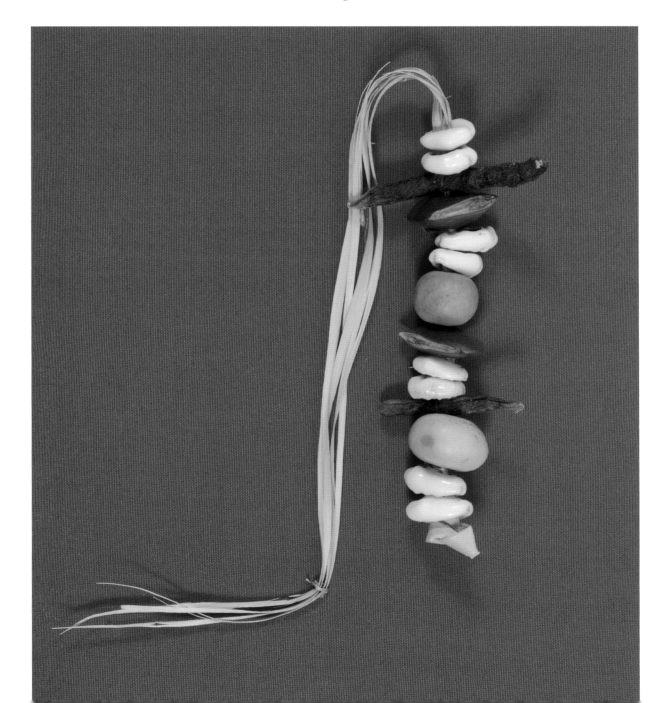

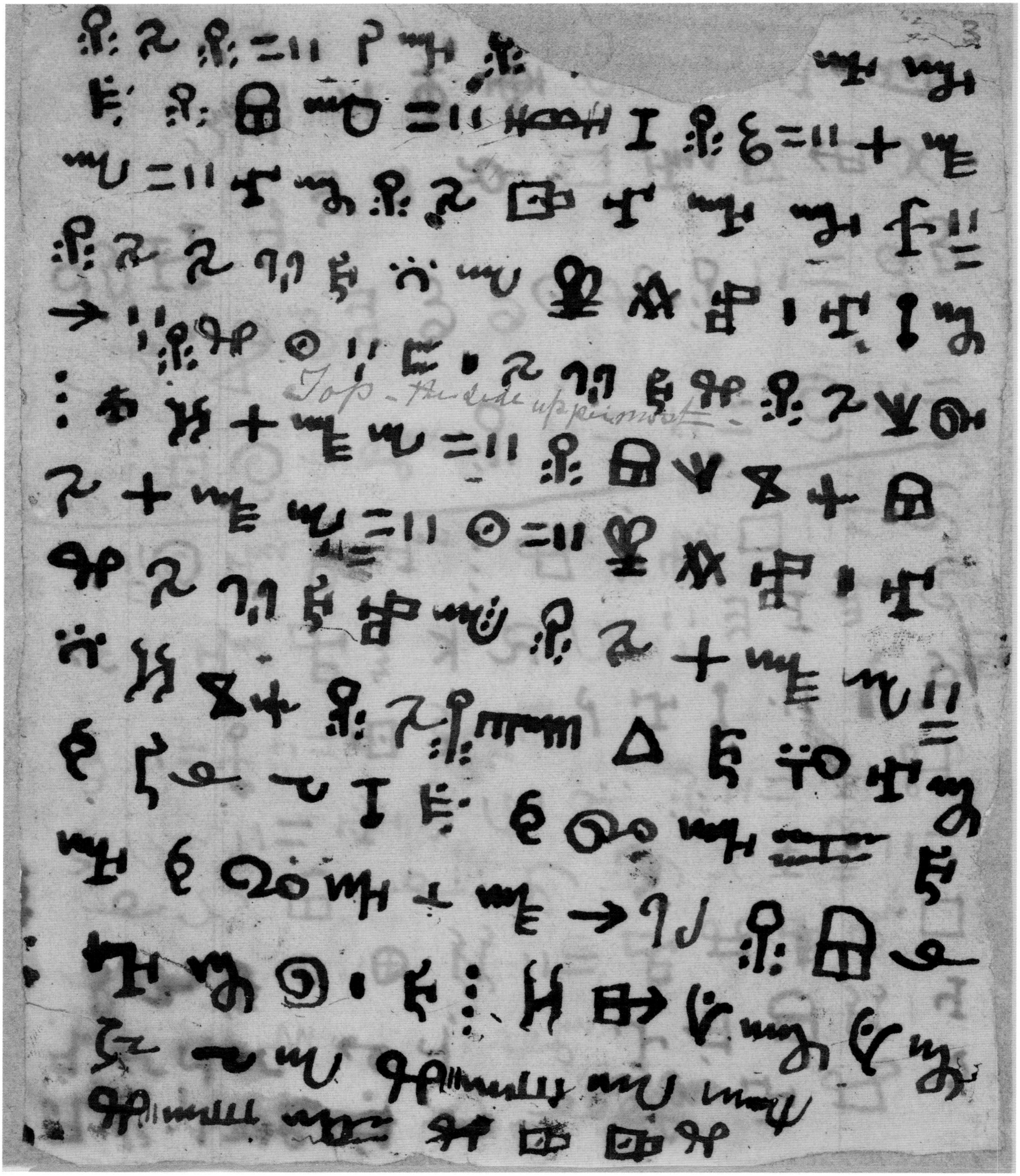
Top - the side uppermost -

Opposite:

This is an early example of the Vai script, collected by a British naval officer, Lieutenant Frederick Forbes, who was stationed off the Liberian coast in 1849.

British Library Add 17817B.

Right:

This wooden carving probably represents a Hausa clerk, from northern Nigeria, employed in the colonial administration. Literacy in English and other Western languages was used to great effect by African writers, but was one option among many as new scripts developed in some areas, and Arabic and Arabic script continued to be used in others.

Nigeria. Before 1947.

British Museum.

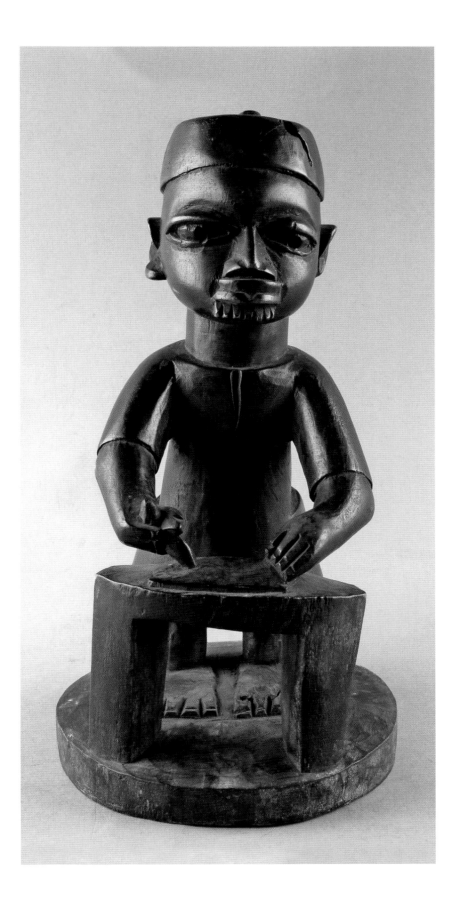

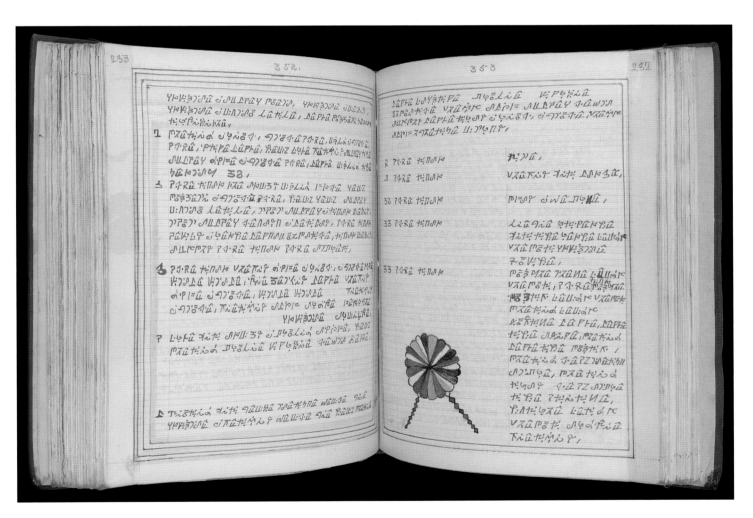

Left:
This is a history book written in the N'ko script. The script has spread widely in Guinea, and has been used in a number of printed books.

British Library.

Below:
Volume one of the *History and Customs of the Bamum People*, written in the secret language invented by King Njoya for use in his kingdom in Bamum, Cameroon. This is the highly valued text *Libonar Pantu Dusang Konik Snak Rifum* (*c.* 1911–18). Shown here is a copy of the original, made by the scribe Nji Mfopu in 1936–8.

Pitt Rivers Museum, University of Oxford.

When he woke up, however, he had forgotten most of the symbols and had to invent new ones. The Vai already used a limited system of pictographs. With the help of friends who were presumably versed in this system, he set about devising a full syllabic script that according to an early scholarly study, not only accurately represents all the sounds in Vai, but also 'phonetically represents English words more accurately than English itself'.[32] Another locally invented script was the pictographic system for writing Bamum created in 1896 by Ibrahim Njoya, king of a Grassfields polity in Cameroon. Like the Vai script, this was allegedly inspired by a dream; and like Bukẹlẹ, Njoya invited other people to help him contribute to the script, and then gradually reduced a collection of almost 400 signs to a more manageable eighty. The Bamum script was taught in schools and used at court for administrative and political communications; it was also used to record the kingdom's history and document local customs and knowledge.[33]

Both these scripts are associated with a desire for self-expression beyond the confines of writing systems brought from outside, and link closely to claims to local identities and to the dignity of precolonial African kingdoms. Similar ideas were present in the case of N'ko, invented in the late 1940s by Souleymane Kanté of Kankan, Guinea, to write Mande languages. Kanté was the son of a famous Qur'anic teacher and was himself well versed in Arabic literacy. After his father's death in 1941, he travelled, read widely and learned other languages. Reportedly he was provoked into creating N'ko when he encountered the view that Africans were inferior because they had no writing of their own. N'ko script was alphabetic, not syllabic or pictographic, and Kanté's aim was to promote widespread grassroots literacy in the Mande-speaking area. He encouraged formerly illiterate Mande speakers to use it to write down their own ideas and memories, and wrote many works himself, which were duplicated and disseminated by travelling merchants: these included a translation of the Qur'an, a 4,000-year history of the Mande world, local histories and writings on the customs and culture of the Mande. Kanté was thus one of the champions of a Mande cultural nationalism 'from below', aimed at empowering ordinary people by providing easy access to literacy and by encouraging the use of writing to preserve local traditions and knowledge in Mande languages.[34]

Conclusion

The literatures described in this chapter offer windows onto different moments of West African creativity during more than a century of literary writing, and over a much longer period of oral composition and the creation and elaboration of rich visual symbols and textual practices. Whether pan-African or local in orientation, West African authors often emphasise the cultural integrity of Africans and the necessity not to let go of the past. From Blyden to Casely-Hayford to Nkrumah and Achebe, the public is constantly reminded that the continent's history stretches back long before colonialism. Yet, at the same time, the authors of this period were astonishingly inventive and creative, forging a new consciousness and creating texts that cast a searing light onto the present and formed a launchpad to a better future.

Endnotes

1   'Praise' poetry is typically addressed to a subject whose aura and reputation it enhances. It is not necessarily flattering: rather, it evokes subjects' potential and hails their distinctive characteristics. It may even include allusions to embarrassing or shameful incidents as long as they are memorable. Addressed to a chief or king, praise poetry may also subtly reprimand the subject by alluding to the ideal behaviour expected of them.

2   Not all African authors did so, of course; Chapter 5 discusses 'modern' African literature more generally.

3   E. W. Blyden, *West Africa before Europe and Other Addresses Delivered in England in 1901 and 1903* (London: C. M. Phillips, 1905) p. 132.

4   J. E. Casely Hayford, 'Introduction', in Blyden, *West Africa before Europe*, p. iv.

5   Kwame Nkrumah, *Towards Colonial Freedom: Africa in the Struggle against World Imperialism* (London: Heinemann, 1962), p. x. This pamphlet was written in 1942 but Nkrumah could not find a publisher willing to print it for another twenty years.

6   Nkrumah, *Towards Colonial Freedom*, p. 44.

7   J. E. Casely Hayford also wrote non-fiction, including books about African systems of government, law, land tenure, and the value of indigenous institutions. See, e.g., *Gold Coast Native Institutions* (London: Sweet and Maxwell, 1903).

8   J. E. Casely Hayford, *Ethiopia Unbound: Studies in Race Emancipation* (London: Frank Cass, 1911; reptd 1969), p.147 ff.

9   Blyden, *West Africa before Europe*, p. 101.

10 Chinua Achebe, *There Was a Country: A Personal History of Biafra* (London: Allen Lane, 2012), p. 54.

11 Kwame Nkrumah, *Autobiography* (Edinburgh: Thomas Nelson, 1957), p. vii.

12 Blyden, *West Africa before Europe*, pp. 135–7.

13 From *Poems of a Black Orpheus*, trans. William Oxley (London: The Menard Press, 1981), p. 18.

14 Léopold Sédar Senghor, 'L'esprit de la civilisation ou les lois de la culture négro-africaine' in *Présence Africaine*, special issue, *Le 1ᵉʳ Congrès International des Écrivains et Artistes Noirs*, 8–10 (1956), p.56. 'Engagés' is translated as 'committed' in the English translation of this edition (also *Présence Africaine*, 8–10 (1956)).

15 Amílcar Cabral, *Our People Are Our Mountains: Amilcar Cabral on the Guinean Revolution* (Committee for Freedom in Mozambique, Angola and Guiné, 1974), p. 15.

16 Amílcar Cabral, *Return to the Source: Selected Speeches* (New York and London: Monthly Review Press, 1973), p. 60.

17 Cabral, *Return to the Source*, p. 60.

18 Cabral, *Our People Are Our Mountains*, n.pag.

19 R. Okonkwo, enlarged by J. Abiakam, *Never Trust All That Love You* (Onitsha: J. C. Brothers Bookshop, *c*. 1975, earlier ed. 1961), pp. 18; 9.

20 Chukwuma 'Kaduna' Nzeogwu (1937–1967) was born and raised in Kaduna, northern Nigeria, where many Igbos lived.

21 Nnamdi Azikiwe, 'Lamentation', in *Civil War Soliloquies* (Nsukka: African Book Company, 1977), pp. 38–40.

22 Christopher Okigbo, 'Hurrah for Thunder', *Collected Poems* (London: Heinemann, 1986), p. 94.

23 Emmanuel Obiechina, 'Foreword', in Chinua Achebe, Arthur Nwankwo, Samuel Ifejika, Flora Nwapa *et al.*, *The Insider: Stories of War and Peace from Nigeria* (Enugu: Nwankwo-Ifejika and Co., 1971), p. vi.

24 Obiechina, 'Foreword', p. vi.

25 Flora Nwapa, *Never Again* (Enugu: Tana Press, 1975), back cover.

26 Nwapa, *Never Again*, back cover.

27 Azikiwe, *Civil War Soliloquies*, p. v.

28 Achebe, *There Was a Country*. Achebe joined the Biafran Ministry of Information at the outbreak of the war as a diplomat and fundraiser. He was unable to write fiction for twenty years after the end of the conflict.

29 Christine Mullen Kreamer, Mary Nooter Roberts, Elizabeth Harney and Allyson Purpura, 'Inscribing Meaning: Writing and Graphic Systems in African Art', *African Arts* 40 (3), 2007, pp. 78–91.

30 Adolph Hilary Agbo, *Values of Adinkra and Agama Symbols* (Kumasi: Bigshy Designs and Publications, 2006).

31 Ọlatunji Ọpadọtun, *Àrokò* (Ibadan: Vantage Publishers 1986).

32 August Klingenheben, 'The Vai Script', *Africa* 6 (2), 1933, pp. 158–71 (quote on p. 166).

33 Kreamer *et al.*, 'Inscribing Meaning'.

34 Dianne White Oyler, 'The N'ko Alphabet as a Vehicle of Indigenist Historiography', *History in Africa* 24, 1997, pp. 239–56.

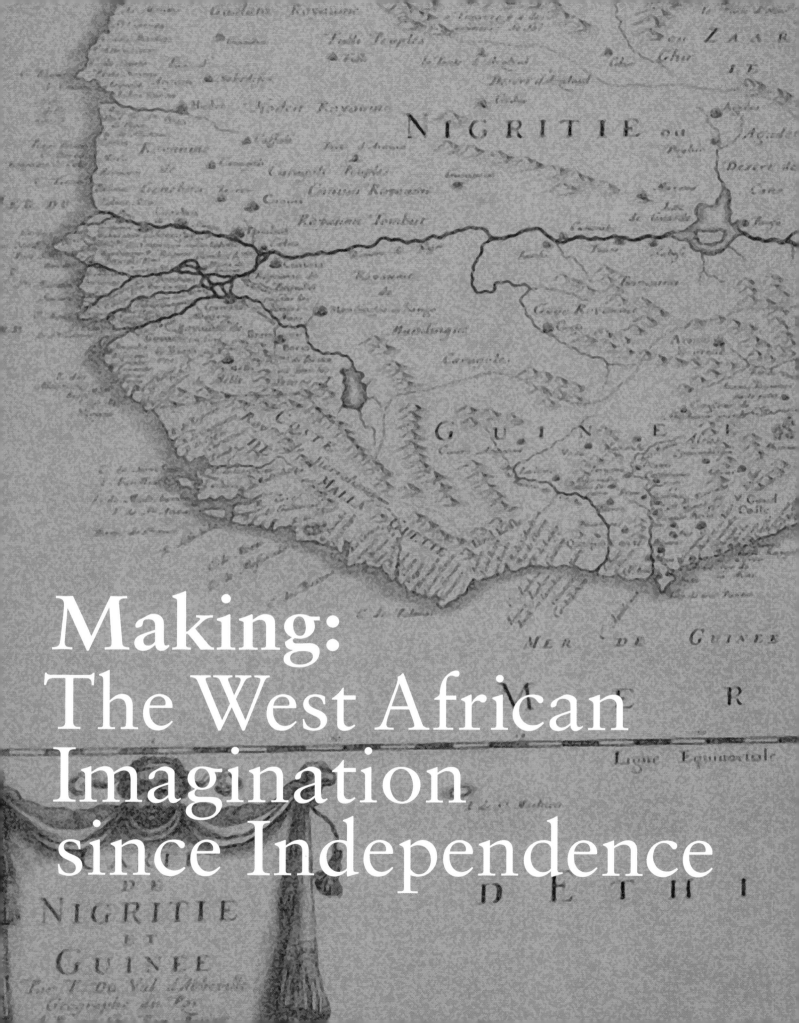

Making:
The West African
Imagination
since Independence

CHAPTER

FIVE

PIUS ADESANMI

Beginnings: Modernity and the West African Text

The Kenyan writer and scholar Ali Mazrui famously described the African present as a product of 'Africa's triple heritage'. Modern or post-colonial Africa, he argued, was formed by its own cultures and civilisation on the one hand, and the cultures and civilisation of both the Arab/Islamic and the Western Judeo-Christian worlds on the other. Needless to say, the last two are foreign intrusions. Taken together, they represent the continent's encounter with the historical violence of imperialism, spelled out through conquest, enslavement, colonialism and neocolonialism.

If Africa today – including its politics, culture and identities – is a product of this triple heritage, nowhere is this more evident than in literature, especially in its expanded meaning of the totality of the creative genres (art, music, film) that the literary scholar Francis Abiola Irele refers to as 'the African imagination'.[1] Modern West African literature, from its earliest emergence to its phase of cultural nationalism in the 1950s and 1960s and its phenomenal flowering thereafter, is best understood as an imaginative scribal and textual world shaped by Africa's triple heritage. West African oral literature – orature – is mostly associated with the traditions, cultures and worldviews of precolonial or pre-contact Africa. The Arabic/Islamic heritage is associated with a significant portion of the written literatures of the West African Sahelian region, and the Western/Judeo-Christian heritage has shaped the literature written in English, French and Portuguese.

The phrase 'modern African literature' is now convention-ally used to describe fiction and creative non-fiction written in the languages of European colonialism, which in West Africa means mainly English and French. It should not be forgotten, though, that a written creative literature developed in African languages such as Yoruba and Twi both before and after independence. The literature in European languages emerged in the first half of the 20th century, and has its basis in Africa's contact with Europe. The use of the term 'modern' to describe this European-language corpus has met with criticism from scholars and commentators because of the ideological environment into which this literature was born. English and French are languages of colonial humiliation and imperial dispossession. They are the languages in which Europe imagined, constructed and inscribed an 'Africa that never was', to borrow the title of a famous 1970 book that explores in detail four centuries of racist fictioning of Africa and the African in European writing.[2] The language issue raises questions: Does the 'modern' in 'modern African literature' imply that West African writing in European languages is superior to that in African languages? Where does oral tradition stand in relation to the modern? If only texts in European languages are described as modern, does this lend weight to Eurocentrism?

Beyond language considerations, generations of African writers have been shaped by the politics and the socio-cultural ambience of the era in which they came of age. For the foundational writers from the early 20th century to the era of independence in the 1960s, the dominant agenda was to conceptualise art as the cultural arm of pan-Africanism, political nationalism, decolonisation and other forms of Black/African radical agenda. A second generation responded to the tensions occasioned by the unravelling of the dreams of independence in and after the 1960s. Women's writing was born into this context and began to challenge the patriarchal slant of the male tradition in literature. This era of disillusionment has yielded to the contemporary era of the African text, where a new generation of writers across the continent is being inserted into the transnational predilections of global or world literatures. The practices of this new generation of post-2000 writers are further amplified by the new global cultures created by social media. African writing today is as much the novel that is being bought in a conventional bookshop in Lagos or London as it is the Kindle edition being ordered in Sydney; it is as present in the tweets of Teju Cole as it is in the Facebook flash fiction of Chuma Nwokolo and Lola Shoneyin.

Oral Tradition

As elsewhere in the continent, West African oral tradition is made up of a wide range of specialised verbal art forms: proverbs, riddles, chants, folk tales, myths, legends, epics, wisecracks and song are the repository of a community's core values, philosophies, mysteries, rituals and memory. Oral tradition is the ultimate culmination of what the Nobel Prize-winning Nigerian author Wole Soyinka calls 'the African world'.[3] A people's oral tradition bears their worldview, way of life, stories and memory. It is a window into what they thought of as beauty and ugliness, and how they expressed such sentiments.

It is performance that, above all, characterises oral tradition in West Africa – a tradition that survives and evolves from one generation

Cloth made in commemoration of Chinua Achebe after his death in 2013.

British Library.

to the next through transmission by word of mouth. Oral literature exists only in the moment of its re-creation, as the performer draws on material from collective ancestral lore familiar to the audience and gives it a distinctiveness from his or her own reserves of innovation, delivery, inventiveness and command of language. An oral enactment is revelry in which performer and audience jointly 'own' the text, reworking it in a call and response format.

West African oral tradition made its entry into the world of 20th-century written cultures on two levels. On one level, it served as a source of inspiration and material for the writers who, starting from roughly the 1950s, would produce the novels, plays and poetry in English and French that we now call (modern) West African literature. In form as in content, the West African imaginative text as we know it today is a hybrid of oral tradition and Western influences. Writers such as Amos Tutuola, Chinua Achebe, Wole Soyinka and Ben Okri owe much to oral tradition. Following in the footsteps of the famous Yoruba-language novelist D. O. Fagunwa, who mined the resources of the Yoruba mythological world of the dead and the unborn, Tutuola published famous novels in English in the 1950s in which the Yoruba world of spirits, ghommids[4] and other surrealist characters is made to interact with the world of the living. Chinua Achebe's great achievement in *Things Fall Apart* (1958) is the creation of a domesticated English language that carries the oral flavour and profundity of the Igbo language. Wole Soyinka employs the same strategies in his plays.

On a second level, oral tradition, while continuing to flourish and develop as an oral form, is now also part of West African written culture in its own right. The introduction of Western literacy made possible the collection, transcription and publication of oral traditions in African languages and in English and French. Many of West Africa's foundational producers of literature in European languages were also involved in the collection and publication of orature. In 1947, the Nigerian novelist Cyprian Ekwensi published *Ikolo the Wrestler and Other Igbo Tales*. Chinua Achebe was also involved in the collection, transcription and publication of Igbo folk tales. For example, in 1973, he co-authored *How the Leopard Got His Claws*. Francophone West African writers were quicker off the mark than their anglophone counterparts in this field. The Ivorian novelist and poet Bernard Dadié published his own collection of folk tales, *Le pagne noir* (*The Black Cloth*), in 1955, while Senegal's Birago Diop published two volumes, *Les contes d'Amadou Koumba* (*The Amadou Koumba Tales*), which were collected by the author from the griot Amadou Koumba and transcribed into French. They are extensive human and animal tales of various ethnic groups in Senegal, especially the Wolof. In general, these stories follow the classic African folk-tale pattern, in which human and animal characters are involved in

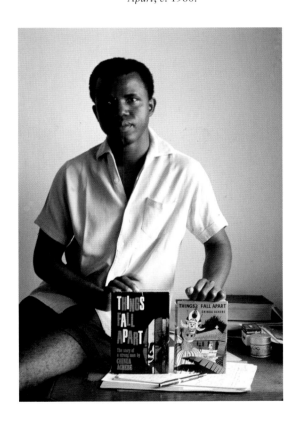

Chinua Achebe holding two editions of his novel *Things Fall Apart*, *c*. 1960.

HOW THE LEOPARD GOT HIS CLAWS

BY CHINUA ACHEBE AND JOHN IROAGANACHI
WITH THE LAMENT OF THE DEER BY CHRISTOPHER OKIGBO

intrigues that serve to explain socio-political phenomena. The misfortunes of such characters serve as a lesson to society.

Beyond the folk tale, early modern West African writers also devoted considerable attention to the collection and transcription of sagas, epics and other genres. In 1960, the Guinean writer Djibril Tamsir Niane published *Soundjata ou l'epopée du Mandingue* to global critical acclaim. Translated into English as *Sundiata: An Epic of Old Mali*, as noted in Chapter 1, this text has become, arguably, West Africa's most translated epic. In Nigeria, the playwright John Pepper Clark published *The Ozidi Saga* in 1977.

Committing oral literatures to paper had consequences for oral tradition in West Africa. Folk tales, proverbs, riddles and epics collectively owned by specific peoples began to appear in books and publications that were, according to Western convention, ascribed to individual authors and editors; genres of oral tradition began to answer to the names of collectors and transcribers. Conscious of this awkward situation, African writers have often insisted on being presented by publishers and editors as translators and transcribers of collective genius. For instance, the original edition of *The Ozidi Saga* published by Ibadan University Press and Oxford University Press gives John Pepper Clark as editor and translator.

Written Literature

Written literature in Africa can be argued to extend as far back as 5,000 years. Commentators in the Afrocentric school of thought usually trace it to the scribal traditions of ancient Egypt. They also emphasise the importance of the Arabic poetic tradition, which began roughly with the Arab conquest of Egypt in the 7th century; the spread of that tradition to the Maghreb and, eventually, to West Africa from the 9th century; and the later development of Hausa Islamic/Arabic verse, which began to be written in northern Nigeria/southern Niger from the 17th century.[5]

These ancient traditions and trajectories notwithstanding, it is generally acknowledged that the first West Africans to produce what is usually understood as modern written literature were survivors of the slave trade living in the diaspora of Europe, such as Olaudah Equiano and Ignatius Sancho (discussed in Chapter 3). Written literature in Africa south of the Sahara proper, especially West Africa, emerged in the late 19th century, and developed gradually in the first half of the 20th century (see Chapters 2 and 4). Missionaries established schools and codified the writing of local languages, thus paving the way for indigenous-language literatures to flourish. The above-mentioned Yoruba fiction of Nigeria's D. O. Fagunwa is a good example.

However, European language literature is the dominant branch of African literature. Colonial violence and the socio-political damage it caused constitute the background to West African literature in English and French. Writers and texts have, however, developed over the decades in complex and varied ways and have explored a whole range of different themes and ideas from a multiplicity of standpoints. There is, nevertheless, a crucial divide between anglophone and francophone politics, which has strongly influenced writers and given direction to their creative vocation. For francophone West African writers, the ideology was the Negritude movement founded in France in the 1930s; for their anglophone counterparts, it was cultural nationalism. Both ideologies would produce the literatures of protest and resistance that dominated the 1950s and 1960s. The writers of this foundational generation plunged into Africa's reservoir of culture and tradition to forge a mytho-ritualistic centre and basis of identity which could energise new narratives to counter five centuries of European racist misrepresentation.

Negritude was an intensely political and cultural ideology. Coming to an awareness of their own blackness in the world, the Negritude poets made an aesthetic effort – through their writing – to retrieve this blackness from centuries of racism. Racial pride came hand in hand with pride in the status of Africa as the matrix of civilisation and culture, which had been violated by enslavement, colonialism and other historical crimes. It was the duty of the Negritude poet to return to this African cultural source.

From its origins in the 1930s until it began to wind down in the 1950s, Negritude poetry was the medium through which modern African literature came to international attention. One of the founding fathers of the movement, and arguably its most prolific theoretician, was Léopold Sédar Senghor, first president of Senegal.[6] The thematic preoccupations of West African Negritude poets such as Senghor,

Covers of the ground-breaking journal *Black Orpheus* (1958 and 1959). *Black Orpheus* described itself as 'a journal of African and Afro-American literature' and published a wide range of creative writing and literary criticism. It was founded in 1957, published in Nigeria and edited by, among others, Wole Soyinka and the South African writer Es'kia Mphahlele.

David Diop, Birago Diop and Bernard Dadié would feed into the work of an entire generation of West African francophone novelists in the 1950s to 1970s.

Poetry comparable in stature to Negritude poetry did not come out of anglophone West Africa until the 1960s to 1980s, with the publication of works by Sierra Leone's Abioseh Nicol and the Nigerians Wole Soyinka and Christopher Okigbo, just to mention three. If Negritude poetry went back to a source it mythologised as 'Mother Africa' for the aesthetic purpose of reclaiming a positive racial and cultural identity, the foundational modern poetry of anglophone Africa – anthologised memorably in Donatus Nwoga's *West African Verse* (1967) and Soyinka's *Poems of Black Africa* (1975) – essentially took up the same themes, but with a deeper concern for incorporating African myths, beliefs and legends into the process of retrieving African identity and culture. This is the essence of cultural nationalism.

We see this in the exploration of the *abiku* motif by Wole Soyinka and John Pepper Clark in their respective poems of the same title, 'Abiku'. In the Yoruba world, abiku is a spirit-child condemned to repeated goings and comings between the world of the living and the dead. Such a child is a source of great torment for a mother who is condemned to repeated childbirths. Only sacrifice and propitiation of deities can break the endless cycle of birth and death enacted by an abiku child. In the Igbo world, the abiku is known as *ogbanje*, as we see in Ezinma, the daughter of Okonkwo, the hero of Achebe's *Things Fall Apart*. In his Booker Prize-winning novel *The Famished Road*, Ben Okri portrays the protagonist, Azaro, as an 'abiku'.

The novel came of age in francophone West Africa from the 1950s, when writers such as Mongo Beti, Camara Laye, Ousmane Sembène and Cheikh Hamidou Kane,[7] along with their counterparts from Central Africa and other francophone outposts in the continent, arrived on the scene. In many instances, this foundational generation of novelists continued where Negritude poetry had left off. The thematic preoccupations of the greatest West African francophone novels of the 1950s and 1960s are the existential impasse created for Africans by the clash of tradition and modernity; colonialism and its regimes of violence; the erosion of Africa's values; and the vagaries of life in colonial and post-colonial cities. Many of these novels became classics in English translation and appeared in Heinemann's African Writers Series. They included Ferdinand Oyono's *Une vie de boy* (*Houseboy*), which tells the story of the tragedy of the colonial encounter through the eyes of Toundi, a child protagonist, growing up in colonial Cameroon. Toundi turns his back on his parents, his culture and Africa, and embraces the white man and his religion. He becomes an altar boy in a colonial setting of European missionaries, teachers and colonial civil servants. By throwing him into the world of European colonial expatriates in Africa, the novel exposes the hypocrisy of the myth of Europe's superior civilisation. Through Toundi's probing eyes, the world of the Europeans is exposed: they are racists; they sleep with each other's spouses; they steal; they tell lies; they drink in excess; and their Christianity is shown up for its false piety. For all his devotion to the Europeans, they end up killing Toundi because of the colour of his skin.

Many of the francophone novels of this era are variations on this theme of colonial violence and European hypocrisy, delivered with irony, sarcasm, satire and trenchant *humour noir* – and Marxist angst in the case of Ousmane Sembène. Yambo Ouologuem, however, would become famous for charting a different and radical course that was revolutionary for its time. In *Le devoir de violence* (1968), he revisits Africa's precolonial past, not in the usual gesture of painting

Amos Tutuola, *The Palm-Wine Drinkard*, 1952.

British Library 003696197.

it as glorious, but to expose the seamy underbelly of that history in a way that no African writer had ever done. The romanticisation of African history that was the standard fare of Negritude poetry was discarded and replaced with a past of violence and barbarity.

However, for all the success of the West African novel in French in the 1950s and 1960s, it was Chinua Achebe's *Things Fall Apart* (1958) that placed African fiction in the ranks of the 20th-century greats. Although Amos Tutuola's *The Palmwine Drinkard*, published in 1952, and Cyprian Ekwensi's *People of the City*, published in 1954, had both attracted considerable critical attention, *Things Fall Apart* was the event, the moment, when African literature really took off. The novel quickly became the signal text of cultural nationalism and remains Africa's most famous work of fiction to date. In *Things Fall Apart*, the epic dimension of Africa's contact with Europe, a preoccupation of much of modern African literature, reaches its philosophical and aesthetic peak. Okonkwo is the eponymous African tragic hero of the colonial encounter. He is an Igbo alpha male who has succeeded in his society through industry and hard work. His world falls apart when Europeans arrive on the scene and impose new ways of being and seeing. His culture is a pragmatic one and begins to adapt to these changes, but Okonkwo is inflexible. He opposes colonial rule and increasingly becomes alienated from his people and the very culture he is defending. Unable to resolve these contradictions, he strikes one last blow against the white man's messenger and commits suicide. Much of anglophone West African fiction explores versions of the multiple themes tackled by Achebe in his works, from *Things Fall Apart* to his last novel, *Anthills of the Savannah* (1987), either as collective socio-political fissures in a changing world or as individual dramas of alienation. Cyprian Ekwensi, Elechi Amadi, Ayi Kwei Armah, Kofi Awoonor, Wole Soyinka and others[8] all wrote major novels in English in the 1960s to 1980s. Ayi Kwei Armah, however, departs from the Achebe template in *The Beautyful Ones Are Not Yet Born* (1964). Although Armah takes on the question of post-colonial disillusion and the unravelling of the dreams of independence as Achebe had done in *A Man of the People*, published in 1966, Armah adds a transcendental, universalist dimension to the theme of post-colonial failure. Unlike the preceding tradition in which we encounter named heroes like Okonkwo and Toundi, Armah's hero is The Man. His peregrinations in Accra, the Ghanaian capital, are cast as something like a voyage into the nascent post-colonial rot of an African setting: these are gripping descriptions of human faeces, mucus and phlegm on walls of public buildings, and an abundance of garbage. Such is the hyperbolic investment in scatology that the text assaults the visual and olfactory senses of its readers.

West African drama is perhaps the genre that has connected most effectively to oral tradition, because the two are close in form:

Left:
Wole Soyinka's *The Lion and the Jewel*, produced at the University of Ibadan, Nigeria, 1964.

British Library Peggy Harper Collection C1074.

African religious and spiritual performances – rituals, sacrifices, festivals, funerals, christenings – are forms of drama, and constitute the roots of modern theatre in West Africa. In francophone West Africa, playwrights have engaged with themes ranging from the recuperation of history and historical figures to neo-Negritude exploration of colonialism, resistance and post-colonial despotism. In anglophone West Africa, Wole Soyinka and a host of other playwrights published plays exploring the full range of human experience within the cosmic order and within the contexts of colonialism, neo-colonialism and the self-inflicted tragedies of the African post-colonial order.

Soyinka's plays, the most notable of which are *A Dance of the Forests* and *Death and the King's Horseman*, explore the entire range of these thematic preoccupations. Mystical, dense and complex, the former mines the riches of Yoruba myth and spiritualities to predict and forewarn against the political tragedies that set in quickly after Nigeria's independence in 1960 and eventually led to the civil war of 1967–70. *Death and the King's Horseman* is the culmination of Soyinka's vision of an existence in which mythology, tradition and deities intrude into the secular predilections of humanity in a colonial context.

Opposite:
Wole Soyinka's play *Death and the King's Horseman* performed at the National Theatre, London in 2009.

In Chinua Achebe's *Things Fall Apart* and *Arrow of God*, we encounter Okonkwo and Ezeulu as models of African heroism whose own hubris combines with the machinations of the colonial order to produce the tragic hero. But Elesin Oba's tragedy in *Death and the King's Horseman* is a product of personal failure and the play of mythological forces drawn from both Greek and traditional Yoruba tragedy. Elesin Oba (literally, the King's Horseman) is the king's chief servant, fated to commit suicide upon his master's death, for a king in the old Yoruba kingdom of Oyo in southwest Nigeria does not 'travel alone' to the world of the dead. To this ritual suicide of Elesin Oba the community attaches the imperative of cyclical communal cleansing and rebirth. To fail to commit suicide in this context is to imperil the entire community. The British colonisers think that the practice is barbaric. Of course! And they intervene at a most inauspicious moment in the arrogant manner of colonisers to stop that which, according to a character in the play, they 'do not understand'. Elesin Oba capitalises on the ignorance of the white coloniser to abdicate his own ritual responsibility. Such is the premium Soyinka places on this mix of mythology, tragedy, failure and the betrayal of duty that, in his author's note, he warns critics not to interpret the play simply in terms of the straitjacket of a culture clash between Europe and Africa.

Across West Africa, a new generation of writers began to innovate in theme and style in the 1970s. The West African writers who came of age in the 1970s shifted their gaze from Negritude and cultural nationalism to life in the post-colony as, all over Africa south of the Sahara, the rejoicing at independence from European colonialism yielded to chaos, corruption, military coups, civilian tyranny and one-party authoritarian states. The transition from independence euphoria to post-independence disillusionment inaugurated a thematic shift in African literatures that is beautifully summed up by the literary critic Neil Lazarus as 'great expectations and the mourning after'.[9] Literature began to look inwards to explore the incipient post-colonial rot.

In francophone West Africa, this shift from colonial critique to post-colonial angst led to a focus on state power and its authoritarian apparatuses of oppression. Francophone West African novelists of the 1970s and 1980s were obsessed with this theme, and this led to the emergence of an extensive corpus of dictatorship novels, launched by Alioum Fantouré's *Le cercle des tropiques* (*Tropical Circle*) (1973). This novel deftly sets up the shift from colonialism to post-colonial horror, as we witness the end of the colonial administration and the advent of the post-colonial incubus in the shape of a tyrant and a draconian one-party state apparatus.[10] The prevalence of the dictatorship tradition in francophone African fiction (in West Africa and beyond) is perhaps not a surprise. After all, this is the region of Africa south of the Sahara that produced a long list of presidents-for-life or presidents who were pushed out after ruling with a heavy hand for several decades: memorable examples include Gnassingbé Eyadéma of Togo, Modibo Keïta of Mali, Mathieu Kérékou of Benin and Seyni Kountché of Niger.

In anglophone West Africa, the split by the generation of the 1970s – the so-called second generation – came in the form of bitter critical disagreements that pitched Wole Soyinka of the first generation against a group of Marxist writers and intellectuals who accused him of literary obscurantism. As was the case in francophone Africa, the joys of independence had unravelled. From Ghana to Nigeria, Sierra Leone and Liberia, and in countries beyond West Africa, the democratic space had all but disappeared, to be replaced with military despotism or civilian authoritarianism. The ground was being prepared for civil wars and the collapse of the nation-statist idea. And the stage was also being set for the neo-colonial takeover of the continent by the IMF and the World Bank and the structural adjustment programmes that exacerbated widespread poverty and starvation in the 1970s and 1980s.

Against this background, writers such as Niyi Osundare, Ken Saro-Wiwa and Femi Osofisan[11] subscribed to a revolutionary vision of art deployed in the service of the people. This art had to be able to raise the consciousness of the masses, and not to alienate them. In prose, their writing expressed the urgency of the post-colonial condition and the need for art to faithfully record the condition of the people. This explains why social realism became the dominant form of creative literary expression, and would remain uninterrupted until the publication of Ben Okri's *The Famished Road* in 1991. The plays of the Nigerian writer Tunde Fatunde are instructive in this respect. *Oga na Tief-Man*, *Water No Get Enemy* and *Blood and Sweat*, were all published in the mid-1980s. Written in pidgin English, the language of the masses, the plays boast a Marxist-revolutionary plot in which the people rise against their domestic oppressors and their Western puppet-masters.

Besides Fatunde's plays, two other books also exemplify the themes, ideologies and textual strategies of the generation of the 1970s and 1980s. Festus Iyayi's novel *Violence* (1979) and Niyi Osundare's collection of poems *Songs of the Marketplace* (1983) reflect the desire to be the voice of the masses, to write a poetics of social revolution; both authors won the Commonwealth Prize for Literature. The violence in Iyayi's novel is the metaphorical violence of poverty created in post-colonial Africa by the rapacious ruling classes that replaced the colonial masters. The book was hailed as Nigeria's first truly proletarian novel, as it explores the world of low-income wage earners in a capitalist economy dominated by the rich and their access to corrupt money. The novel's hero literally has to sell his blood to make ends meet. What Iyayi does in prose, Osundare does in poetry, expressing what claims to be the voice of the ordinary people, of peasants, of the oppressed. His titles – such as *Songs of the Marketplace*, *Village Voices* – embody this concern.

Ben Okri belongs to this second generation of Nigerian writers, although he was not a participant in the Marxist literary rebellion of the 1980s. Unlike the other writers in his generation, he has spent much of his life in London and hardly articulates a conscious politics of African identity. He became world famous after winning the Booker Prize for his novel *The Famished Road* in 1991. His major contribution was to create a space for the surreal and the fantastic in an era when his peers in Africa were investing in easily accessible realism in their creative texts as a way of rooting their art in the life-world of ordinary people. After Tutuola's novels and Wole Soyinka's *A Dance of the Forests*, West African literary surrealism or magical realism had gone into hibernation, with the Ghanaian novelist Kojo Laing remaining its only notable practitioner. Okri's *The Famished Road* inaugurated a return to magical realism, handled in a way that did not alienate his text from the social concerns of his generation. The book is the story of Azaro, an abiku or spirit-child growing up in an unnamed city in Nigeria. The spirit world and the real world constantly meet and clash in this fantastical narrative and Azaro's gaze on the ghetto in which he lives with his impoverished parents reveals the post-colonial rot of urban poverty and dispossession.

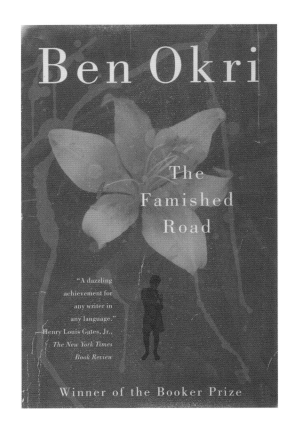

Ben Okri, *The Famished Road*, 1991.

Women's Writing

On the whole, African women arrived on the literary scene much later than their male counterparts. Although there was the occasional female presence in the anglophone and francophone poetic currents of the 1940s and 1950s, cultural impediments to the education of women, coupled with the Western sexism of the colonial system, kept girls out of the earliest missionary schools and ensured that female writing in the sense of a sustained tradition and a corpus did not really take off until after the 1960s. Flora Nwapa's novel *Efuru*, published in 1967, was anglophone West Africa's first major novel by a woman; in francophone Africa, the Cameroonian Thérèse Kuoh-Moukoury was the first to publish a novel, *Rencontres essentielles* (*Essential Encounters*), in 1969. However, the 1970s and 1980s witnessed an explosion of writing by women such as the anglophone Buchi Emecheta, Zulu Sofola, Ama Ata Aidoo, Efua Sutherland, Ifeoma Okoye, Zaynab Alkali and Osonye Tess Onwueme, and, in francophone countries, Aminata Sow Fall and Mariama Bâ.

Women's writing arose out of the desire to introduce a female perspective into the socio-political vision of Africa portrayed by male writers, and to address women's experience and the cultural

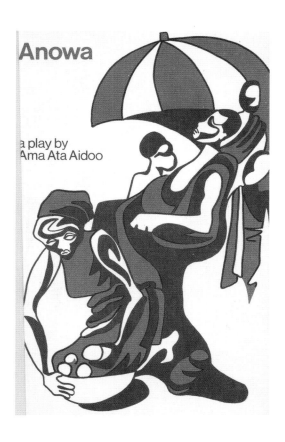

Ama Ata Aidoo, *Anowa*, 1970.
British Library X.908/20281.

barriers they faced. Also, women now had the means and will to write. The head start that West African male writers had over their female counterparts meant that they could narrate Africa as a site of male power, will and desire. The ideological revision of history, the platform on which the African writer supposedly challenged Empire, produced heavily gendered accounts of Africa's historical victimhood and agency. Colonialism, for instance, became the site of a clash between the men of Europe and the men of Africa. This explains why a long list of heroes – Okonkwo in *Things Fall Apart*, Ezeulu in *Arrow of God*, Samba Diallo in *L'aventure ambigue*, Elesin Oba in *Death and the King's Horseman* – constitutes Africa's tableau of fictional resistance to colonialism. That these heroes were mostly destroyed also depicts Africa's victimhood as a male affair.

African women writers created a wide range of themes to counter this masculinist account of Africa's encounter with modernity. The position and role of women as mothers and daughters within the institution of marriage, especially polygamy, the difficulties imposed by social and traditional expectations of women, female genital mutilation and gender inequality are all themes explored in female-authored texts that became African literary classics in the 1970s and 1980s. In Flora Nwapa's novel *Efuru*, for instance, the eponymous heroine breaks a long chain of male heroes in anglophone West African fiction. And because the novel is set in the same precolonial bucolic Igbo world as *Things Fall Apart*, it offers a female perspective on many of the same cultural issues.

Where Igbo women had been nothing more than marginal textual foils in Achebe's book, their world becomes the centre of Nwapa's work and their voices are at the heart of the construction of communal order. Efuru is unlucky in her attempts at marriage in a socio-cultural context that frowns on the unmarried woman and blames her for the associated condition of childlessness. Efuru defies these gender constrictions in a traditional Igbo setting and focuses with considerable success on her commerce and her role as a spiritual mother figure who undermines codifications of her gender by patriarchy. Focus on the female subject's voice and perspective is also evident in the plays of the Ghanaian Efua Sutherland. In *Edufa* – and in other plays – she employs a deft marriage of Greek and Ghanaian mythologies to focus on the female experience. However, the centring of the female experience would acquire a more radical and strident tone in Buchi Emecheta's *The Joys of Motherhood* and Ama Ata Aidoo's *Our Sister Killjoy*. In *Our Sister Killjoy*, Aidoo writes an experimental text that combines prose and poetry to explore the world of a Ghanaian woman, Sissie, who travels to Europe on a fellowship and bonds with a white German woman, Marija, in a lesbian relationship. The relationship is uneasy, as both women have to cross cultural, racial, political and other boundaries.

Flora Nwapa (1931–1993), author, publisher and commissioner for health and social welfare in Nigeria's East Central State in the 1970s.

Zulu Sofola's *The Wizard of Law* performed in Abuja, Nigeria, 31 October 2012.

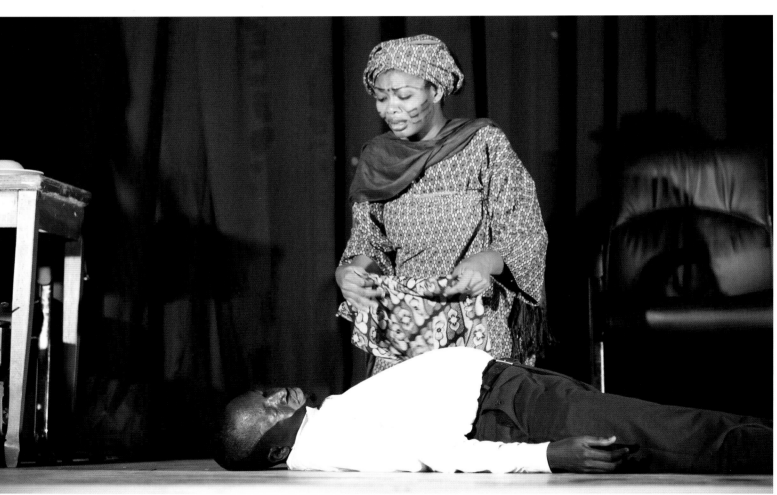

Women's issues or feminism was not an obligatory theme for the female writers of this generation. A good number of Zulu Sofola's plays, especially *King Emene*, explore themes of power, and political and social injustice. Although Tess Onwueme's play *What Mama Said* offers a cast of revolutionary women, it is more political than feminist. The terrorised and pauperised inhabitants of a fictional setting confront severe repression by the state and multinational oil companies. The reference to the struggles of the people of Nigeria's oil-rich Niger Delta region is palpable.

In francophone West Africa, Mariama Bâ's two novels, *Une si longue lettre* (*So Long a Letter*) and *Un chant écarlate* (*Scarlet Song*), placed francophone African women's writing on the international literary map. Translated into English, they became quasi-manifestos of African feminism because of their trenchant handling of the female experience in marriage and tradition. With two of her novels, *La grève des battu* (*The Beggars' Strike*) and *Ex-père de la nation*, Aminata Sow Fall, a Senegalese contemporary of Mariama Bâ, introduced to female fiction the sort of pro-masses social realism that had hitherto been associated with the work of Senegalese male writers, notably Ousmane Sembène in the novels *Xala*, *Le mandat* (*The Money-Order*) and *O pays, mon beau peuple*.

Children of the Post-colony

A new generation of West African writers emerged in the mid-1980s, but did not gain international recognition until a decade later. Most of them were born in the 1960s to 1980s, after colonialism had ended in much of the continent. They were therefore not witnesses to the historical events that had shaped the themes and ideological direction of earlier generations. The political reality of these writers is that of the failed African post-colony struggling with domestic challenges to the very idea of statehood on the one hand, and with the pressures of globalisation, transnationalism and diasporic flows on the other. In an influential essay, the French–Djiboutian novelist Abdourahman Waberi described this new generation of writers as 'the children of the post-colony';[12] they would later come to be known as 'migritude writers'. 'Migritude' is a contraction of the words Negritude and migrancy, a hint of the fact that many of these writers were either born, or are based in, France, and have produced a new corpus of African novels rooted in the immigrant tradition.

West African contributors to migritude literature are largely writers from Togo and Senegal, notably Fatou Diome, Sami Tchak and Kossi Efoui. Fatou Diome's *Le ventre de l'Atlantique* (*The Belly of the Atlantic*) handles the theme of an immigrant's search for identity in Paris with considerable brio, while Sami Tchak's *Place des fêtes* examines the contradictions and dilemmas of being African in Paris: born in France of African parentage, yet not quite French because of social stereotypes and assumptions about identity.[13]

In anglophone West Africa, the origins of third-generation writing can be traced to the explosion of poetry in the two Nigerian literary hubs of Ibadan and Nsukka in the 1990s. This significant shift in Nigerian letters was signalled by the publication in 1988 of Harry Garuba's *Voices from the Fringe*, an anthology of poems that assembled the work of new writers who would go on to dominate the Nigerian and, indeed, the West African literary scene throughout the 1990s.[14] These poetic works belong to a tradition that mostly captured the frustrations of the moment. Given the fact that Nigeria's second phase of military rule lasted from 1983 to 1999, this generation of writers had their formative years determined by repression and the suppression of freedom and individual liberties under military despotism. As undergraduates, they witnessed the gradual collapse of the Nigerian university system. They wrote in a state of siege.

It was not all poetry in the 1990s phase of West African writing. Omowunmi Segun, Akin Adesokan and Maik Nwosu published their novels, *The Third Dimple*, *Roots in the Sky* and *Invisible Chapters* respectively. Chuma Nwokolo, Sola Osofisan and Biyi Bandele also published novels. Bandele relocated to London and become the first member of this generation to attract international attention after publishing a string of successful plays and novels through the 1990s.

Third-generation West African writing took off internationally after 2000, when Nigeria's Helon Habila won the Caine Prize for African Writing in 2001 for his work *Waiting for an Angel*, which tells the story of Loomba, a young journalist living in Lagos under military dictatorship in the 1990s – just like Habila and the generation of writers under consideration. The Caine Prize introduced the world to new African writers who had previously had only localised attention in the capitals of their respective countries. Even writers who did not win the Caine Prize did not really escape the practices of valuing, privileging and canonising African writing on the transnational stage it had inaugurated. The Nigerian Prize for Literature comes with a winner's cheque of US $100,000, and guarantees for its winner the sort of prestige and visibility accorded African winners of foreign prizes such as the Caine Prize.

Hence, whereas the first wave of West African third-generation writing happened exclusively in Nigeria, the second wave occurred almost exclusively in Euro-America and produced such sensations as Chimamanda Ngozi Adichie, Chris Abani, Teju Cole, Segun Afolabi and Helen Oyeyemi. Significantly, the leading lights of this new writing are almost exclusively women. None of the authors in this new generation comes close to Adichie's status as a world writer who now even features in major betting cycles for the Nobel Prize.

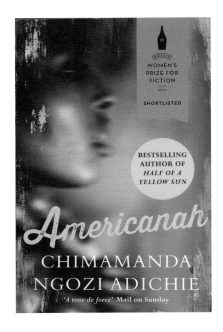

In the novel *Americanah* (2013), Chimamanda Ngozi Adichie examines life and the diasporic experience in the US and Nigeria. Adichie's awards include the Commonwealth Writers' Prize and the Orange Prize.

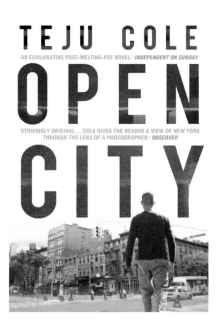

Above:
Helon Habila, *Waiting for An Angel*, 2002.

Above right:
Teju Cole's *Open City* has won numerous prizes. It deals with a young Nigerian–German psychiatrist living in New York in the wake of 9/11.

However, her fellow Nigerians Chika Unigwe, Lola Shoneyin and Adaobi Tricia Nwaubani have also become established international novelists in their own right. Shoneyin's novel *The Secret Lives of Baba Segi's Wives*, a bold, surprising take on female agency and rebellion in the context of polygamy, has been translated into several languages. Unigwe's *On Black Sisters' Street*, which tackles the trafficking of African women for prostitution in Europe, has also enjoyed tremendous success. Nwaubani's *I Do Not Come to You by Chance* is the most famous fictionalisation of the '419' phenomenon of internet scam letters.[15]

Recently, a new literature has emerged that is shaped almost exclusively by gadgetry and social media. Vibrant new writers, mostly in their twenties, have already produced significant work in prose, poetry and drama that is becoming increasingly visible locally and internationally. This is especially true of anglophone West Africa in general and Nigeria in particular. These writers have developed a very keen sense of themselves as a new literary generation. Although they have published novels, plays and poetry in the traditional book format, writers such as Richard Ali, Tolu Ogunlesi, Paul Liam, Ukamaka Olisakwe and Abubakar Adam Ibrahim are very active online and are constantly pushing the boundaries of the West African text and releasing large amounts of creative fiction on social media. Some of these writers have been nominated for international literary prizes. On Facebook, on Instagram, on Twitter, they produce flash fiction and flash poetry daily, and this body of work is engaged with by their peers across the continent and in Euro-America. With this generation, will the West African imagination remain literature or will it become Twitterature?

Endnotes

1   F. Abiola Irele, *The African Imagination: Literature in Africa and the Black Diaspora* (Oxford: Oxford University Press, 2001).

2   Dorothy Hammond and Alta Jablow, *The Africa That Never Was: Four Centuries of British Writing about Africa* (New York: Twayne, 1970).

3   Wole Soyinka, *Myth, Literature and the African World* (Cambridge: Cambridge University Press, 1976).

4   'Ghommid' is a term for Yoruba supernatural beings.

5   See the chapter 'The Growth of Written Literature in English-Speaking West Africa', in Emmanuel Obiechina, *Language and Theme: Essays on African Literature* (Washington: Howard University Press, 1990). Obiechina makes a strong argument for considering the Arabic script and other African-language scripts such as nsibidi as the true origins of written literature in West Africa.

6   For Senghor see also Chapter 4.

7   Other important West African francophone writers at this time included Ferdinand Oyono, Seydou Badian, David Ananou, Ahmadou Kourouma, Yambo Ouologuem, Alioum Fantouré and Tierno Monenembo.

8   They included Isidore Okpewho, Gabriel Okara, T. M. Aluko, Onuora Nzekwu, John Munonye, Festus Iyayi, Kole Omotoso and Abubakar Gimba.

9   Neil Lazarus, 'Great Expectations and the Mourning After: Decolonization and African Intellectuals', in Neil Lazarus, *Resistance in Postcolonial African Fiction* (New Haven: Yale University Press, 1990).

10 Other classic examples of dictatorship novels include Williams Sassine's *Le jeune homme de sable*, Tierno Monenembo's *Les crapauds-brousse* (*The Bush Toads*), and Ahmadou Kourouma's *En attendant le vote des bêtes sauvages* (*Waiting for the Wild Beasts to Vote*).

11 Other writers of this school included Festus Iyayi, Tunde Fatunde, Odia Ofeimun, Tanure Ojaide and Bode Sowande.

12 Abdourahman Waberi, 'Les enfants de la postcolonie: Esquisse d'une nouvelle génération d'écrivains francophones d'Afrique noire', *Notre Librairie*, 135, 1998, pp. 8–15.

13 Among famous non-West African migritude writers are Waberi, Alain Mabanckou, Daniel Biyaoula, Bessora and Leonora Miano.

14 Significant collections from this phase of West African writing include Olu Oguibe's *A Gathering Fear*, Nduka Otiono's *Voices in the Rainbow*, Remi Raji's *A Harvest of Laughters*, Uche Nduka's *Chiaroscuro*, Ogaga Ifowodo's *Homeland and Other Poems* and Lola Shoneyin's *So All the Time I Was Sitting on an Egg*.

15 These scam letters are named after Section 419 of the Nigerian Criminal Code, which deals with fraud.

Further Reading

The British Library's collections of materials relating to West Africa are rich and varied. For audio and audio-visual materials, consult the catalogue at http://www.bl.uk/ and filter by 'audio'. Also explore selected West African collections at http://sounds.bl.uk/World-and-traditional-music and http://sounds.bl.uk/Arts-literature-and-performance. For books, pamphlets, newspapers, journals and maps search the catalogue at http://www.bl.uk/.

Introduction

Emmanuel Akyeampong (ed), *Themes in West Africa's History* (Athens, OH: Ohio University Press, 2006)

J.F.A. Ajayi and Michael Crowder, *History of West Africa*, 3rd ed. (Harlow: Longman, 1985)

Karin Barber, *The Anthropology of Texts, Persons and Publics: Oral and Written Culture in Africa and Beyond* (Cambridge: Cambridge University Press, 2007)

Gus Casely-Hayford, *The Lost Kingdoms of Africa* (London: Bantam Books, 2013)

Basil Davidson, *Africa in History: Themes and Outlines* (rev. ed., London: Phoenix, 1992)

Ruth Finnegan, *Oral Literature in Africa* (London: Clarendon Press, 1970)

Carlos Moore, *Fela: This Bitch of a Life* (London: Omnibus, 2010, 1st ed. 1982)

Alan Ricard, *The Languages and Literatures of Africa* (Oxford: James Currey, 2004)

Chapter 1
Building: Narrative and Knowledge in Precolonial West Africa

David Conrad, *Epic Ancestors of the Sunjata Era: Oral Tradition from the Maninka of Guinea* (Madison: African Studies Program, University of Wisconsin, 1999)

Thomas A. Hale, *Griots and Griottes: Masters of Words and Music* (African Expressive Cultures, Bloomington: Indiana University Press, 2007)

John O. Hunwick and Alida Jay Boye, *The Hidden Treasures of Timbuktu* (London: Thames & Hudson, 2008)

Shamil Jeppie and Souleymane Bachir Diagne (eds), *The Meanings of Timbuktu* (Cape Town; Senegal: HSRC Press in association with CODESRIA, 2008)

Graziano Krätli and Ghislaine Lydon, *The Trans-Saharan Book Trade: Manuscript Culture, Arabic Literacy, and Intellectual History in Muslim Africa* (Leiden: Brill, 2011)

T. C. McCaskie, *State and Society in Precolonial Asante* (Cambridge: Cambridge University Press, 2002)

Andy Morgan, *Music, Culture, and Conflict in Mali* (Copenhagen: Freemuse, 2013)

D. T. Niane, *Sundiata: An Epic of Old Mali* (London: trans. G. D. Pickett, Longman, Boston: Boston University Press, 2006)

P. James Oliver, *Mansa Musa and the Empire of Mali* (Createspace, 2013)

Ivor Wilkes, *Asante in the Nineteenth Century: The Structure and Evolution of a Political Order* (Cambridge: Cambridge University Press, 1975)

Chapter 2
Spirit: Histories and Religion of the Word

Wande Abimbola, *Ifa: An Exposition of Ifa Literary Corpus* (Ibadan: Oxford University Press, 1976)

K. Noel Amherd, *Reciting Ifá. Difference, Heterogeneity, and Identity* (Trenton, NJ: Africa World Press, 2010)

K. Noel Amherd and Insa Nolte, 'Religions (West Africa)' in Johnson, D. *et al.* (eds), *Historical Companion to Postcolonial Literatures* (Edinburgh: Edinburgh University Press, 2005), pp. 422–8

Karin Barber, 'Discursive Strategies in the Texts of Ifá and in the "Holy Book of Odù" of the African Church of Òrúnmìlà' in K. Barber and P. de Moraes Farias (eds), *Self-Assertion and Brokerage. Early Cultural Nationalism in West Africa* (Birmingham: Birmingham University African Studies Series, 1990), pp. 196–224

Karin Barber, 'Popular Arts in Africa', *African Studies Review*, vol. 30, no. 3, September 1987, pp. 1–78

William R. Bascom, *Ifa Divination: Communication between Gods and Men* in West Africa (Bloomington: Indiana University Press, 1969)

Louis Brenner, 'Muslim Divination and the History of Religion of Sub-Saharan Africa', in John Pemberton III (ed.), Insight and Artistry in African Divination (Washington and London: Smithsonian Institution Press, 2000), pp. 45–59

Deidre Helen Crumbley, Spirit, Structure, and Flesh: Gender and Power in Yoruba African Instituted Churches (Madison: University of Wisconsin Press, 2008)

H. J. Drewal and M. T. Drewal, Gelede. Art and Female Power among the Yoruba (Bloomington: Indiana University Press, 1983)

Paulo de Moraes Farias, Arabic Medieval Inscriptions from the Republic of Mali. Epigraphy, Chronicles, and Songhay-Tuáreg History (New York: Oxford University Press for the British Academy, 2003)

Jack Goody, 'The Impact of Islamic Writing on the Oral Cultures of West Africa', Cahiers d'Études Africaines, vol. 11, cahier 43, 1971, pp. 455–66

J. F. P. Hopkins and N. Levtzion (eds), Corpus of Early Arabic Sources for West African History (Cambridge: Cambridge University Press, [1981] 2000)

Elizabeth Isichei, A History of Christianity in Africa: From Antiquity to the Present (London: SPCK, 1995)

Babatunde Lawal, The Gèlèdé Spectacle: Art, Gender, and Social Harmony in an African Culture (Seattle: University of Washington Press, 1996)

J. D. Y. Peel, Aladura: A Religious Movement among the Yoruba (London: Oxford University Press, 1968)

Derek Peterson and Giacomo Macola, Recasting the Past: History Writing and Political Work in Modern Africa (Athens, OH: Ohio University Press, 2009)

David Robinson, Muslim Societies in African History (Cambridge: Cambridge University Press, 2004)

Shobana Shankar, Who Shall Enter Paradise? Christian Origins in Muslim Northern Nigeria, ca. 1890–1975 (Athens, OH: Ohio University Press, 2014)

H. W. Turner, History of an African Independent Church. The Church of the Lord (Aladura) (Oxford: Clarendon Press, 1967)

Rudolph T. Ware III The Walking Qur'an. Islamic Education, Embodied Knowledge, and History in West Africa (Chapel Hill: University of Carolina Press, 2014)

Chapter 3
Crossings: Word and Music across the Atlantic

'A Conversation with Stuart Hall', Journal of the International Institute vol. 7, issue 1, fall 1999, http://hdl.handle.net/2027/spo.4750978.0007.107

Kenneth Bilby, Notes to CD 'Drums of defiance: Maroon music from the earliest free Black communities of Jamaica' (Smithsonian/Folkway Recordings, 1992)

Kenneth Bilby, True-born Maroons (Gainesville, FL: University Press of Florida, 2005)

Brycchan Carey, Slavery, Emancipation and Abolition, http://www.brycchancarey.com/index.htm, accessed 13 May 2015

Vincent Carretta, Equiano, the African: The Biography of a Self-made Man (Athens, GA: University of Georgia Press, 2005)

Vincent Carretta and Philip Gould (eds), Genius in Bondage: Literature of the Early Black Atlantic (Lexington: University Press of Kentucky, 2001)

John Cowley, Carnival, Canboulay and Calypso: Traditions in the Making (Cambridge: Cambridge University Press, 1996)

Ottobah Cugoano, Thoughts and Sentiments on the Evil and Wicked Traffic of the Slavery and Commerce of the Human Species, ed. Vincent Carretta (Ann Arbor: University of Michigan Library, 2005)

David Dabydeen and Paul Edwards (eds), Black Writers in Britain, 1760–1890 (Edinburgh: Edinburgh University Press, 1991)

Lucy Durán, 'POYI! Bamana Jeli Music, Mali and the Blues', Journal of African Cultural Studies 25:2, 2013, pp. 211–46

Olaudah Equiano, The Interesting Narrative and Other Writings, ed. Vincent Carretta (London: Penguin, 2003)

Paul Gilroy, The Black Atlantic: Modernity and Double-Consciousness (London: Verso, 1993)

Douglas Grant, The Fortunate Slave: An Illustration of African Slavery in the Early Eighteenth Century (London: Oxford University Press, 1968)

Clarence Bernard Henry, Let's Make Some Noise: Axé and the African Roots of Brazilian Popular Music (Jackson: University Press of Mississippi, 2008)

Gerhard Kubik, Africa and the Blues (Jackson: University Press of Mississippi, 1999) and Cecilia Conway, Africa-banjo Echoes in Appalachia: A Study of Folk Tradition (Knoxville: University of Tennessee Press, 1995)

François Dominique Toussaint L'Ouverture, Mémoires du Général Toussaint L'Ouverture, écrits par lui-même, pouvant servir à l'histoire de sa vie … (Paris: Saint-Denis, 1853). Republished as The Memoir of General Toussaint Louverture, trans. and ed. Philippe R. Girard (Oxford: Oxford University Press, 2014)

Ivor L. Miller, 'A Secret Society Goes Public: The Relationship between Abakua and Cuban Popular Culture', African Studies Review, vol. 43, no. 1 (April 2000), pp. 161–88

Ivor L. Miller, Voice of the Leopard: African Secret Societies and Cuba. Caribbean Studies Series, (Jackson: University Press of Mississippi, 2009)

Mary Prince, The History of Mary Prince: A West Indian Slave, ed. Sara Salih (London: Penguin, 2000)

Jean Rouch, Ciné-Ethnography, ed. and trans. by Steven Feld (Minneapolis: University of Minnesota Press, 2003)

Ignatius Sancho, Letters of the Late Ignatius Sancho, an African, ed. Vincent Carretta (New York: Penguin, 1998)

Arthur Torrington et al. (eds), Equiano: Enslavement, Resistance, Abolition (Birmingham: Equiano Society, 2008)

Understanding Slavery Initiative, http://www.understandingslavery.com/, accessed 13 May 2015

Voyages: The Transatlantic Slave Trade Database, http://www.slavevoyages.org/, accessed 13 May 2015

James Walvin, An African's Life: The Life and Times of Olaudah Equiano, 1745–1797 (London: Cassell, 1998)

Phillis Wheatley, Complete Writings, ed. Vincent Carretta (London: Penguin, 2001)

Chapter 4
Speaking Out: Dissent and Creativity in the Colonial Era and Beyond

Chinua Achebe, There Was a Country: A Personal History of Biafra (London: Allen Lane, 2012)

Chinua Achebe, Arthur Nwankwo, Samuel Ifejika, Flora Nwapa et al., The Insider: Stories of War and Peace from Nigeria (Enugu: Nwankwo-Ifejika and Co., 1971)

Hakim Adi, West Africans in Britain 1900-1960: Nationalism, Pan-Africanism and Communism (London: Lawrence & Wishart, 1998)

Chimamanda Ngozi Adichie, Half of a Yellow Sun (London: Harper Perennial, 2007)

Elechi Amadi, Sunset in Biafra: A Civil War Diary (London: Heinemann Educational, 1973)

Nnamdi Azikiwe, Civil War Soliloquies (Nsukka: African Book Company, 1977)

E. W. Blyden, West Africa before Europe and Other Addresses Delivered in England in 1901 and 1903 (London: C. M. Phillips, 1905)

Amílcar Cabral, Return to the Source: Selected Speeches (New York and London: Monthly Review Press, 1973)

Robert W. July, The Origins of Modern African Thought: Its Development in West Africa during the Nineteenth and

Twentieth Centuries (London: Faber and Faber, 1968)

J. E. Casely Hayford, *Ethiopia Unbound: Studies in Race Emancipation* (London: Frank Cass, 1911; repr. 1969)

J. E. Casely Hayford *Gold Coast Native Institutions* (London: Sweet and Maxwell, 1903)

Adelaide Cromwell, *An African Victorian Feminist: The Life and Times of Adelaide Smith Casely Hayford, 1868–1960* (London: Cass, 1986)

Mabel Dove, *Selected Writings of a Pioneer West African Feminist*, ed. Stephanie Newell and Audrey Gadzekpo (Nottingham: Trent Editions, 2004)

Buchi Emecheta, *Destination Biafra* (London: Allison and Busby, 1982)

Eddie Iroh, *Forty-eight Guns for the General* (Ibadan: Spectrum Books, 1991)

August Klingenheben, 'The Vai Script', *Africa* 6 (2), 1933, pp. 158–71

André Lewin, *Ahmed Sékou Touré, 1922-1984: Président de la Guinée de 1958 à 1984* (Paris: Harmattan, *c.* 2009–*c.* 2011), 8 vols

Firozi Manji and Bill Fletcher jnr (eds), *Claim No Easy Victories: The Legacy of Amilcar Cabral* (n.p.: CODESRIA, 2013)

Christine Mullen Kreamer, Mary Nooter Roberts, Elizabeth Harney and Allyson Purpura, *Inscribing Meaning: Writing and Graphic Systems in African Art* (Washington, DC: National Museum of African Art, Smithsonian Institution, 2007)

Hollis Ralph Lynch, *Edward Wilmot Blyden: Pan-Negro Patriot, 1832–1912* (London: Oxford University Press, 1967)

Stephanie Newell, *Ghanaian Popular Fiction: 'Thrilling Discoveries in Conjugal Life' & Other Tales* (Oxford: James Currey, 2000).

Stephanie Newell, *The Power to Name: A History of Anonymity in Colonial West Africa* (Athens, OH: Ohio University Press, 2013)

Kwame Nkrumah, *Autobiography* (Edinburgh: Thomas Nelson, 1957)

Kwame Nkrumah, *Towards Colonial Freedom: Africa in the Struggle against World Imperialism* (London: Heinemann, 1962)

Saki Mafundikwa, *Afrikan Alphabets: The Story of Writing in Africa* (New York: Mark Batty, 2004)

Flora Nwapa, *Never Again* (Enugu: Nwamife, 1975)

Christopher Okigbo, *Collected Poems* (London: Heinemann, 1986)

Dianne White Oyler, 'The N'ko Alphabet as a Vehicle of Indigenist Historiography', *History in Africa* 24, 1997, pp. 239–56

John Picton (ed.), *The Art of African Textiles: Technology, Tradition and Lurex* (London: Barbican Art Gallery, 1995)

Poems of a Black Orpheus, trans. William Oxley (London: The Menard Press, 1981)

Léopold Sédar Senghor (ed.), *Anthologie de la nouvelle poésie nègre et malgache de langue française* 4th éd.; 1st pub. 1948 (Paris: Presses Universitaires de France, 1977)

Ken Saro-Wiwa, *Sozaboy* (Harlow: Longman, 1994)

Janet G. Vaillant, *Black, French, and African: A Life of Léopold Sédar Senghor* (Cambridge, MA: Harvard University Press, 1990)

Chapter 5
Making: The West African Imagination since Independence

Where possible, recent editions in English (rather than first editions) of creative works are given below. Further suggestions for reading, including titles in French, will be found in the text of Chapter 5.

Chris Abani, *GraceLand* (Johannesburg: Picador Africa, 2004)

Chinua Achebe, *Things Fall Apart*, 1958 (Harlow: Pearson Education, 2011)

Chimamanda Ngozi Adichie, *Americanah* (London: Fourth Estate, 2014)

Ama Ata Aidoo, *Our Sister Killjoy, or, Reflections from a Black-eyed Squint /* (London: Longman, 1977)

Ellah Wakatama Allfrey (ed.), *Africa39: New Writing from Africa South of the Sahara* (London: Bloomsbury, 2014)

Ayi Kwei Armah, *The Beautyful Ones Are Not Yet Born* (London: Heinemann, 1969)

Mariama Bâ, *So Long a Letter* (London: Heinemann, 1981)

Margaret Busby (ed.), *Daughters of Africa : An International Anthology of Words and Writings by Women of African Descent from the Ancient Egyptian to the Present* (London: Vintage, 1993)

The Caine Prize for African Writing, anthologies of short stories by African writers published annually. Details at http://www.caineprize.com/books.php

Teju Cole, *Every Day Is for the Thief* (London: Faber and Faber, 2014)

Bernard Dadié, *The Black Cloth: A Collection of African Folktales*, 1955 (Amherst, MA: University of Massachusetts Press, 1987)

Fatou Diome, *The Belly of the Atlantic* (London: Serpent's Tail, 2006)

Aminatta Forna, *The Memory of Love* (London: Bloomsbury, 2010)

Harry Garuba (ed.), *Voices from the Fringe: An ANA Anthology of New Nigerian Poetry* (Lagos: Malthouse Press, 1988)

Aminata Sow Fall, *The Beggars' Strike, or, The Dregs of Society*, 1979 (Harlow: Longman, 1986)

Alioum Fantouré, *Tropical Circle*, 1972 (Harlow: Longman, 1981)

Dorothy Hammond and Alta Jablow, *The Africa That Never Was: Four Centuries of British Writing about Africa* (New York: Twayne, 1970)

F. Abiola Irele, *The African Imagination: Literature in Africa and the Black Diaspora* (Oxford: Oxford University Press, 2001)

Festus Iyayi, *Violence* (London: Longman, 1979)

Thérèse Kuoh-Moukoury, *Essential Encounters* (New York: Modern Language Association of America, 2002)

Neil Lazarus, 'Great Expectations and the Mourning After: Decolonization and African Intellectuals', in Neil Lazarus, *Resistance in Postcolonial African Fiction* (New Haven: Yale University Press, 1990)

Flora Nwapa, *Efuru* (London: Heinemann Educational Books, 1966)

Adaobi Tricia Nwaubani, *I Do Not Come to You by Chance* (London: Weidenfeld & Nicolson, 2009)

Emmanuel Obiechina, *Language and Theme: Essays on African Literature* (Washington: Howard University Press, 1990)

Ben Okri, *The Famished Road*, 1991 (London: Vintage, 2009)

Chibundu Onuzo, *The Spider King's Daughter* (London: Faber and Faber, 2012)

Ferdinand Oyono, *Houseboy* (London: Heinemann, 1966)

Ken Saro-Wiwa, *Lemona's Tale* (London: Penguin, 1996)

Ousmane Sembène, *God's Bits of Wood*, 1962 (Oxford: Heinemann, 1995)

Ade Solanke, *Pandora's Box* (London: Oberon Books, 2012)

Lola Shoneyin, *The Secret Lives of Baba Segi's Wives* (London: Serpent's Tail, 2010)

Wole Soyinka, *Death and the King's Horseman*, 1975 (London: Bloomsbury, 2015)

Wole Soyinka, *Myth, Literature and the African World* (Cambridge: Cambridge University Press, 1990)

Wole Soyinka, *Selected Poems* (London: Methuen, 2001)

Efua Sutherland, *Edufa*, 1967 (London: Longman, 1979)

Amos Tutuola, *The Palm-wine Drinkard and His Dead Palm-wine Tapster in the Deads' Town*, 1952 (London: Faber and Faber, 2014)

Chika Unigwe, *On Black Sisters' Street* (London: Jonathan Cape, 2009)

Abdourahman Waberi, 'Les enfants de la postcolonie: Esquisse d'une nouvelle génération d'écrivains francophones d'Afrique noire', *Notre Librairie*, 135, *1998, pp. 8–15

Index